THE
PRINCIPLES
OF
PUBLIC
RELATIONS

THE PRINCIPLES OF PUBLIC RELATIONS

Revised Edition

Harold Oxley

KOGAN
PAGE

First published in 1987 by
Kogan Page Ltd,
120 Pentonville Road, London N1 9JN

Revised paperback edition, 1989

British Library Cataloguing in Publication Data

Oxley, Harold
  The principles of public relations.
  1. Public relations
  I. Title
  659.2   HM263

ISBN 1-85091-394-3 (Hbk)
ISBN 1-85091-984-4 (Pbk)

Printed and bound in Great Britain by
Biddles Ltd, Guildford and King's Lynn

Contents

Preface

With good reason those who work in public relations are called practitioners: public relations is a practice. But it is not a haphazard practice, it is planned. Plans are based on principles which, in this book, are taken to be generalities derived from observation and assumed to be true.

The emphasis of this book is on the priorities of public relations and the principles that underlie them. Thus it is a clear step removed from the level of how-to-do-it. There are therefore no tables of statistical data, no checklists, no references to current costs or existing technologies. These things change continually; priorities and principles are relatively stable. The author has also tried to distance himself from the social and cultural specifics of any particular country. However, principles are largely derived from practice and practice inevitably takes place in a social and cultural context. No doubt therefore, the author's Canadian-English-American background shows through in the illustrative material. Nevertheless, the main thrust is on a higher level of generality.

Ethical principles are not dealt with. The book is limited to the operational principles that underlie standard public relations practice. The ethical principles of public relations are stated explicitly in various national and international codes of conduct. The operational principles, however, generally have to be inferred either from the way practitioners operate or from textbook descriptions of their approach. When one does that and then carefully examines the exposed principles, most seem clearly reasonable but some appear to need refinement and a few seem opposed to those of other disciplines.

The first purpose of this book is to make explicit the main principles of standard practice. To do this, the nature of public relations is examined, then each of its operational phases—situation analysis, setting objectives, planning and evaluation—is analysed separately. In the final two chapters the same style of examination focuses on two other principle-guided aspects of public relations—specialized public relations and training for public relations. As the underlying principles are successively made explicit, the defensible ones are supported, those that need refinement get some, and those that seem misguided are questioned without apology.

The principles themselves appear in italics, each in its context within the body of the text. They are listed in full in Appendix 1.

The book is intended primarily for practitioners and students of public relations. It should also prove helpful to people engaged in public relations either casually or temporarily. Some familiarity with the fundamentals of public relations would be helpful but is not necessary to an understanding of the text.

1. The Nature of Public Relations

Public Relations—Science or Technology?

'We are very sorry but we cannot guarantee results.' It would be legitimate, I think, to read this apology into Clause 9 of the British Institute of Public Relations' *Code of Conduct*:

> 'A member shall not negotiate or agree terms with a prospective employer or client on the basis of payment contingent upon specific future public relations achievements.'

The defence of this clause usually hinges on three arguments:

(1) public relations performance cannot be evaluated by results achieved over a given period of time, for example, the duration of a contract;
(2) public relations achievement cannot be evaluated solely by measurable results;
(3) extraneous factors can affect the attainment of public relations objectives.

A fourth defence should be considered: public relations deals more often with probabilities than with certainties, but guarantees can be based only on certainties.

As a rule, the most a practitioner can say on launching a project is, 'I hope this works. I think it will, but I can't be sure.' Public relations is not simply the cut-and-dry application of a set of foolproof principles, it is an exploration of human relationships. The practitioner is guided by what he knows but every time he faces a new situation he also faces the possibility and necessity of learning more. The continuing search to learn more can be guided only by a combination of known certainties and interesting probabilities. It is not that the practitioner puts his client at risk by indulging his own curiosity rather than banking on what can't miss; there are simply not enough certainties to eliminate all the risks. The practitioner works to eliminate uncertainties, but he can do that only by pursuing probabilities. It is an approach with

1

respectable credentials in the sciences and it is one that makes very good sense.

A scientific approach

One can draw a parallel with a medical researcher trying to find a cure for a disease. He begins by studying the situations in which the disease exists, and those who suffer from it, in order to form an understanding of its origins and the factors that sustain or aggravate it. He then proposes an explanation. He is not sure of it; it is a well informed, respectable guess. He must therefore test it by applying a possible remedy which, if his understanding of the disease is correct, should cure it. If the disease remains he will at least have learned that his explanation must be questioned— an important lesson. If the disease disappears he will have more confidence in his explanation. He still cannot be sure of it; perhaps something else accounted for the disappearance of the disease but at least his proposed explanation will have gained strength through the test. He may think of several ways to test his explanation. If it survives each test he might get to the point where he has enough confidence in it to accept it without further testing. This would not be a confirmation of its absolute truth, but a declaration of respect for its probable truth. From then on he could concentrate on developing ever-more-effective cures for the disease. In this way, slowly but surely his understanding of the disease and its control would grow.

One takes the same approach to solving public relations problems. The practitioner begins by analysing the situation to get a comprehensive view of the problem. What seems to have caused it? What aggravates it? What are its ramifications? Eventually he develops a plausible explanation for it. Unless it appears to be a problem in every way identical to one he has seen before (which is very unlikely) he finds himself in the position of the medical scientist: he has to test his explanation. To do this he proposes a solution—a public relations project of some kind. However, since his explanation is tentative he cannot at this point be sure that his proposed solution will eliminate the problem. He should have enough confidence in it to defend his proposal but if you put the straight question to him: 'Are you 100 per cent certain that this project will succeed?', he would have to admit that its total success was only probable. The suggested explanation is therefore a hypothesis and the proposed solution is designed to test its validity.

Assuming that the project was well designed and carefully implemented, if it fails to eliminate the problem the practitioner will have good reason to question his understanding of the situation. If on the other hand the problem is eliminated at the end of the project, he will have more confidence in his explanation but will still not be absolutely sure of it. He will be able to say only that his efforts probably solved the problem. It remains possible that it was eliminated by factors of which he was unaware.

The point must be made here that not all public relations activities are directed to solving problems. Continuing programmes are more often designed to maintain favourable relationships already established between organizations and their publics. However, the approach does not change. The practitioner is forever testing either his comprehension of the existing relationships or how he tries to preserve them. And in either case, as with problem-solving, he is dealing only with probabilities. But if he persists, gradually the probabilities will strengthen and eventually they will lead him to the discovery of principles.

Public relations and science

The public relations practitioner clearly has less control over his experiments than a researcher in a laboratory but his method is essentially the same. It is a systematic approach to acquiring and evaluating information. It is a method that searches for explanations derived from observable evidence, and although based on probabilities, it tries to establish firm bases for prediction. However, the fact that the public relations practitioner uses a scientific method is not enough to classify him as a scientist. Science is characterized by two main elements: one is its systematic method, the other is its goal. The goal of science is to identify the principles which govern the subject being studied, in particular, previously unknown principles. It is in this sense that science tries to expand the horizons of human knowledge. To discover the principles that underlie a phenomenon is to enrich one's comprehension of the phenomenon itself and to open the way for further exploration. If one has grasped the principles one can apply them to new situations, delimiting their scope and testing their strength. This is why scientific statements (principles, assertions, hypotheses, theories etc) must always be testable. No matter how plausible a statement may seem, if it cannot be tested there is no way to determine its possible contribution to science. What is more, the results of scientific tests must be reliable. That is to say, the outcome of a test must be such that it could be obtained by anyone, anytime, anywhere, as long as the test was carried out under prescribed conditions. If the observed result has to be qualified, the qualification must be made explicit.

3

For example, it is not scientifically accurate to say that water boils at 100 degrees Celcius. One should add that it boils at that temperature only at sea level and then only if it is pure water.

Notice that science is not restricted to any particular subject matter, for example the physical universe which interests physicists and chemists. Science can just as legitimately deal with cultural phenomena or human and social behaviour. Since the subject matter is not the determining factor, the study of physics can be unscientific and the study of mysticism scientific. It depends on the goal pursued and the method employed. What about public relations, then? Could it be considered a science? Certainly its subject matter—the relationships between organizations and their publics (those groups of people with whom organizations interact)—would be a legitimate scientific interest, and the approach taken by practitioners in their work could, as we have seen, be interpreted as a scientific method. But it is not clear that public relations has a scientific goal. The practitioner is primarily interested in establishing and maintaining a sort of congeniality between his organization and its publics. Since this, as a planned activity, depends on the application of principles, the practitioner is of course interested in principles. But whereas a scientist is primarily interested in the discovery of principles, the public relations practitioner is more concerned with their application.

Public relations and technology

Given that the application of scientific knowledge to practical ends is technology rather than science it would seem that, based on current practice, public relations would more accurately be called a technology than a science. But should it be so? Think again of the medical profession. A medical practitioner is one whose main concern is the application of scientific principles to the benefit of his patients. He is therefore a technologist. The medical researcher, on the other hand, occupies himself with the discovery of principles which will later be applied in the practice of medicine. The necessary link between practice and research is as clear as the distinction between them. In the case of medicine the distinction is emphasized by the fact that the two functions are often performed by different people. In public relations the situation is different. The practitioner occupies himself with the application of principles, but where does he get them? Many of them he finds in other disciplines, for example psychology, mass communication, sociology, political science or business administration. But significantly, they are *other* disciplines. Whatever principles they have to offer to public relations were derived from different fields of study. The danger in borrowing them is not that they might prove second-rate but that even collectively they will not serve public relations adequately.

Public relations research

Public relations research does go on in universities but how much of it is pure research of a type that discovers new principles? Some of it is directly related to the problems of organizations that have commissioned it and a lot is library research of principles already discovered. Moreover, very little of it is solely related to public relations. It could just as well be considered research in mass communications, business administration, sociology or some other discipline. This is not to denigrate such research; it is extremely important but it is not enough. Yet there is not a distinct and recognizable body of public relations professionals whose first responsibility is to discover the special principles related to their field of interest. In other words, there are no pure scientists in public relations, only applied scientists—technologists—practitioners. By default it is left to them to discover whatever unique principles underlie their work. If there is such discovery it is a secondary outcome of their practice, something that most often occurs in the evaluative stage of a project. Pure scientific research would be carried out in advance of project planning, indeed independently of it. It must therefore be said that the current practice reflects a principle that *public relations functions as a technology rather than a science*. The scientific knowledge it applies in its practice is gleaned from other disciplines and public relations practice rather than from independent research.

This principle might very well be called into question in the near future. The impact of new technologies (cf Chapter 7) on social and industrial structures will put unprecedented demands on those responsible for the relationships between organizations and their publics, and conceivably we could see the forced emergence of what would amount to a new field of scientific inquiry—public relations. The process of scientific inquiry can be triggered by any number of stimuli—an unforeseen side effect or even the failure of an experiment, a consequence of some form of behaviour, an implication of an already verified principle, or (as perhaps in public relations) the pressure of changing circumstances. In any case, the response is more important than the stimulus.

Systematic, Intuitive and Creative Public Relations

Of the numerous definitions of public relations currently in circulation, none is universally accepted. Most came into being as statements of what practitioners actually do. Later the more durable of them became statements of what practitioners should do. However, since none of them is supported by sanctions, even the most widely accepted ones are in fact nothing more than statements of what public relations practitioners sometimes do, could do, would find it helpful to do, are advised to do or expected to do (by whom?). The practitioner, therefore, is more precisely directed in his work by the terms of his contract than by academic definitions of public relations. He might, however, benefit from considering some of the definitions if only to provide himself with a fresh point of reference. A definition which is someone else's view of how the job could or should be done can be sparkling enlightenment to a practitioner immersed in the urgencies of his practice.

The public relations practitioner

The public relations practitioner functions between the management of the organization which employs him and all other internal and external groups or individuals with which his organization has anything to do. The organization may be a commercial business, a public service, a voluntary organization, a football team, a trade union, a rock group or even an individual person. Those with whom the organization deals—an equally diverse assembly—are usually termed 'publics', no matter how many or few people each of them comprises. One person could be a public. It is the job of the practitioner to help things go well between his organization and its publics. He is either a fully employed member of his organization or an external consultant working on contract. Understandably therefore, in spite of his intermediary function between the organization and its publics he is inevitably more closely identified with the organization. He frequently, in fact, becomes its spokesman. He therefore makes it his business to thoroughly understand its structure, objectives, policies, practices, strengths and weaknesses. To the degree that it is considered by management to be necessary, he then makes this information publicly known. He is not thereby functioning as a leak; rather, he serves as a respectable informant. At the same time, he tries in whatever ways he can, to get to know the publics with which he is dealing. He is interested in anything which might bear on their relationships with the organization—their composition, living and working conditions, beliefs, attitudes, hopes, fears, expectations, behaviour etc. Here again, he evaluates this information and makes relevant items known to his employer. In this way, without compromising his role as a representative of the organization, he functions at the same time as an unofficial delegate of the organization's publics. At times this second function even leads him to recommend policy changes in the organization to the benefit of the publics. His purpose in serving both the organization and its publics is to create a base of mutual understanding on which the two parties can build a solid and positive relationship. Not surprisingly, the pursuit and maintenance of mutual understanding figures prominently in many definitions of public relations.

But the practitioner's job rarely stops there. He is frequently required to promote the organization's interests through campaigns of one kind or another. This sometimes leads to confusion between the roles of public relations and advertising or marketing in commercial organizations. A key difference is that while advertising and marketing are directly concerned with the sale of products and services, public relations seeks to create the public dispositions that will make sales promotion effective. In public relations, more than in advertising and sometimes more than in marketing, two-way communications is therefore the rule. Furthermore, the public relations practitioner takes a broader approach in his work than do those whose principal concern is the flow of products or services. It can happen that a public relations problem exists while the demand for an organization's goods or services remains strong. For example, in communities where the police are vilified for brutality or discrimination (definitely a public relations problem), the demand for their services does not weaken. Any breakdown in the rapport between an organization and its publics is a public relations problem whether or not it directly affects the organization's observable functions. The problem may be linked to social or cultural traditions, environmental conditions, ethical systems, aesthetic tastes or historical tensions. It may relate to public beliefs or ideologies, the repercussions of public experience, or simply stubborn and irrational behaviour. All of which suggests the complexity of public relations and explains the practitioner's organized approach to his job: if complexity is not managed in an organized way it becomes chaotic.

The public relations process

The practitioner begins, as already pointed out, by analysing the situation to discover its positive and negative aspects, the direction of its evolution, the circumstances impinging on it, its ramifications, the degree to which it is amenable to change and the possibility of its being preserved or strengthened. This can demand a lot of sophisticated research but should not be skimped: situation analysis is too important.

On the basis of his analysis he then decides whether or not to intervene. Sometimes the most advisable course is to leave things alone. If he chooses to take action he first identifies the final objectives he hopes to achieve. To simply wade in and play it by ear is not acceptable practice. In Chapter 3 we will examine in full the setting of objectives; in Chapter 4 each of the planning stages mentioned here will be elaborated. For the moment we will simply sketch the practitioner's systematic approach to carrying out a project.

Guided by his final objectives, he begins detailed planning. This includes identifying all of the publics who will be either affected by the project or involved in it. Since the nature and function of each of these publics will be particular, the practitioner identifies as intermediate objectives what he hopes to achieve in approaching each of them. Clearly, one intermediate objective—an inevitable one—will be to maintain effective communication with each public. As might be expected therefore, 'creating messages', 'selecting communication channels' and 'working with the media' are invariably given high priority in contractual terms of reference and textbook treatments of project planning. What receives far less attention, oddly, is the next step—the justification of intermediate objectives. At this stage the practitioner makes explicit the logical links between his proposed intermediate objectives and the previously established final objectives. Practitioners who overlook this stage sometimes find that they have unwittingly set themselves intermediate objectives that contribute little or nothing to the final purpose of the project.

Then follows a description of precisely how the plan is to be carried out. Things that look impressive in a formal presentation sometimes prove to be impracticable because of the omission of details like 'Who is going to be responsible for this mailing?' or 'How will materials be transported from A to B?'. The practitioner makes all such details clear in his description as well as the scheduling and phasing of each stage of the project. Then the project is costed—in minute detail. Somebody has to pay for it and that person or department naturally wants to know how much is being asked for and why. This is seldom a straightforward task; among other complications, public relations activities are sometimes distributed across a number of different departments.

If the plan in its entirety is approved by all those with authority to pass judgement on it, the project is then implemented. From that point on, the plan becomes a guideline, but not inflexible. Long-running projects must be appraised regularly throughout their implementation. If these periodic evaluations point to a need for revisions, the plan will be appropriately modified in the course of the project. This 'formative evaluation' is distinct from the 'summative evaluation' carried out after the project has been completed.

Continuing programmes

The systematic approach is most succinctly illustrated in the case of a single public relations project, but it applies as well to continuing programmes. In well organized establishments the continuing programme is usually spelled out in two plans—a Strategic Plan, which is somewhat tentative, generally covering a period of three or five years, and a firm Operational Plan for the coming twelve months. As each Operational Plan is approved and budgets allocated the Strategic Plan is re-examined and projected for an additional year so that it always extends a fixed period beyond the Operational Plan. The Operational Plan is naturally the more detailed of the two but both are characterized by the same logical, systematic approach.

The insistence on this approach both in public relations practice and textbook descriptions of it reflects the importance accorded to it. It is considered important for two reasons:

(1) The rationality of the approach, its logical coherence, is considered the surest guarantee of effective performance. This is ultimately a philosophical defence, an affirmation that man works best when he works rationally.
(2) The sequential structuring of standardized phases in the planning and execution of programmes provides a basis for measuring progress, and possibly for assessing performance against that of other organizations.

These two arguments could be slightly recast to express two principles which underlie current public relations practice:

(1) *A rational approach to public relations planning provides the strongest assurance of effectiveness;*
(2) *A systematic approach to public relations planning lends itself to measuring progress.*

The rational approach

Unquestionably a rational plan is always respectable. And usually it is the best assurance the practitioner can get that a programme will be effective. But there is good reason to believe that a stronger assurance sometimes exists. Three terms have to be distinguished: rational, irrational and non-rational. A rational approach is the kind we have just outlined. It is based on the principles and structures of sound reasoning. It reflects the planner's use of his intellect. The final plan is the product of intellectual work, the outcome of a process. A situation has been analysed; facts have been assessed; certain of them have been combined with others to form propositions; propositions have been combined and linked with known principles to form the premises of arguments; conclusions have been drawn and combined with sound ideas to form the intellectual framework for a proposed course of action. It is a process in which feelings, prejudgements and preferences are suppressed. Man, the rational animal, is at work.

The irrational approach

An irrational approach is quite the opposite. Psychoanalysts may recognize patterns of irrational behaviour but as a style of project planning it cannot be described. There are simply too many conceivable variations. But in every case the approach goes against reason. If it can be called a process it is an incoherent one, judged by the standards of rational thought. It may be highly emotional, even compelling, but it is not logically persuasive. It cannot be reasonably defended because it observes none of the principles and respects none of the structures of reasoned thinking.

The non-rational approach

A non-rational approach is every bit as intelligent as the rational approach, but it is not reasoned. The ideas and propositions that emerge from it are not the products of a laborious shaping process comparable to that of the rational approach. They are born intuitively, instantaneously. They bypass the intricate circuitry of reasoning. The intuitive person chooses in a flash a right position, an effective course of action. To those who are not of this type it can seem uncanny, but the intuitive personality is recognized and perfectly respected by psychiatrists who describe it as one in which 'the basic function of intuition dominates.' And intuition, they say, is 'a form of direct cognition ... a rapid analytical understanding of a reference system whose actual analysis would require long discursive development.' (Eysenck *et al*, 1972, p.157) There is convincing evidence in the literature of psychoanalysis that intuitive people often make excellent executives because they take very little time to make sound decisions. Clearly they are not suited to every profession. An intuitive professor would do his students no favour if he bypassed the reasoning process through which his perceptions would normally be discovered. But an intuitive person might very well succeed in public relations. It is a field where the facts required by a reasoning person are sometimes in short supply. And when empirical evidence is lacking, the rational planner has to substitute assumptions which invariably weaken the argument.

The problem with the intuitive person is that his insights cannot be evaluated. Evaluation is a rational process. It doesn't know how to handle the products of intuition. The intuitive executive can be judged only by his performance. Even he himself cannot demonstrate the reasonableness of his propositions; they are not the products of a reasoning process. One has to take a chance on him. But if he has a record of success it is not irrational to have confidence in him. It does not go against reason to respect his judgements. And one cannot rule out the possibility that his judgements will assure the effectiveness of a programme more solidly than would the rational approach. There is a respectable place for intuition in public relations.

Creative public relations

There is place too, just as respectable, for creativity, which may have its origins in intuition alone or any combination of reason and intuition, but is distinguished by its unique products. It goes beyond originality. An original proposal can be defined as one offering a new combination of known principles, known procedures and known facts but going no further. A creative proposal adds something unprecedented.

A creative idea can be inspired by an existing situation, it can find a heritage of reasonableness in arguments that support it, but it goes a step beyond anything previously conceived.

Nothing in the social sciences can match the spectacular outbursts of creative genius that highlight the history of physics, for instance, but in a more modest way these so-called 'soft sciences' are continually advanced by the genius and self-confidence of people who have ventured beyond the limits of what is sure, time-tested and generally accepted. There is no

11

reason why it cannot be so in public relations as well. Certainly, principles that discriminate against intuition and creativity should be re-examined.

The second principle, that a systematic approach helps to measure progress, calls for only two brief comments. First, one should not be led by it to believe that all progress is measurable. Precise measurements depend on data which are either naturally quantified or on which a calibration has been reasonably imposed. Such data are not always obtainable. Still, the systematic approach certainly provides a good framework for comparative evaluation. Remember, though, it does not guarantee that the measurement of 'progress' will always result in a positive value.

Public Relations—A Management Function

That *public relations is a management function* is a principle more explicitly stated than most. But its meaning is not explicit; one has to infer it from the practice or distil it from commentators' various interpretations of the principle. The term 'Management' is sometimes used to refer to a group of people, sometimes to a function. In the former sense it describes those members of an organization with decision-making authority for directing it towards its objectives. In this sense there can be several levels of management, the people with final decision-making authority often being referred to as Top Management. As a function, management is the role exercised by these decision-making people.

In saying that public relations is a management function, let us assume first that the term Management refers to the group of decision makers. Then the expression could mean either (a) that public relations is a role performed by those decision-making people collectively called Management, or (b) it is a role performed for the benefit of those people (Management) by others (non-Management) who are in their service. The difference is important because depending on the interpretation of the expression the public relations practitioner is considered either a member of Management or an outsider at the service of Management. Possibly the preferred interpretation is suggested by the following typical public relations tasks selected from textbooks and contractual terms of reference:

(1) To advise management of all internal and external developments likely to affect the organization's relationships with its publics;
(2) To research and interpret to management, current or anticipated attitudes of key publics towards the organization's affairs;

(3) To act on behalf of management in planning and executing public functions;
(4) To serve as a liaison between management and its publics;
(5) To report regularly to management on all activities in any way affecting the organization's public relationships.

The phrasing of these statements leaves no doubt that those responsible for public relations are to perform a service for the people called Management. That could mean that the public relations practitioner is subject to the authority of Management. But reference is sometimes made to the public relations officer and his 'management colleagues' as though they are equals. If that is so, then to say that public relations is a management function means it is a decision-making role performed by public relations practitioners in collaboration with other Management members. But it is common knowledge that public relations professionals have for decades been complaining that they are not routinely included as members of the board of directors in the organizations which employ them—that they often have no decision-making authority but are simply advisors. Unfortunately there is no consistent policy. This much, however, is clear: the functions performed by the public relations practitioner, whether as a member of the management team or not, are performed for Management. And they are performed to help Management direct the organization to the attainment of its objectives. Consequently the public relations practitioner has no independent self-steering capacity. He is ultimately steered by Management. This does not diminish the importance of his function but it imposes on him a perspective which at times could be too narrow to encompass the full scope of public relations objectives.

Operational style

More commonly his service link to Management steers the public relations practitioner into a restrictive operational style. In most organizations decision makers are committed to an approach based on observable and quantified data. It is a style rooted in the exigencies of private enterprise: organizations must operate within the limits of their own resources and therefore directors take no chances. But data suitable for graphs and flow charts are not always suitable for measuring public relations which must be guided by a broader vision. The cultural context of a situation, the historical setting, even the moral and ethical ambience have to be taken into account in developing a realistic public relations programme. These are not precisely measurable parameters but it is self-defeating to overlook them simply because they lack the snap of quantified data. The assumption in the management approach (when it is applied to public relations) is that you can arrive at an understanding of social phenomena through an inventory of statistical data; but can you? Public relations survey results are typically presented to Management in tables of rows and columns. The rows may represent, for example, educational levels while the columns represent cultural interests. If the table indicates that university graduates prefer print media to television, what does that mean? It is impossible to extricate the significance of that fact. 'University graduates' could include those who studied Secretarial Studies as well as those who studied philosophy; and the category 'print media' could include texts on political analysis and hard-core pornographic magazines. Similarly, economic income brackets are commonly used in statistical analysis. But the category £10,000-£20,000 could include both university professors and hired killers. The ultimate projection from a table of quantified data would be a gigantic paint-by-numbers portrait of the world—impressive, yes, but dead. It would be a portrait based on information rather than knowledge, a mosaic of juxtaposed fragments.

The decision maker argues that the fragments are simply the raw material for interpretation, but his interpretation is limited by the kind of data he has gathered and by the vision that guided his selection. He will generally discover only empirical relationships not logical ones, and he is seldom much interested in theoretical implications. This is hardly surprising and not entirely to his discredit. After all, his organization has to survive in a world of competition. Speed and precision are important to a competitive edge. Subtlety and nuance are amorphous and don't fit neatly into cost-benefit analysis. But it is a restrictive style nonetheless. It may serve the practitioner in his capacity as a Management functionary but it is inadequate for independent public relations practice.

Public Relations for Intellectuals

Effective public relations is effective communication—a principle frequently expressed negatively: a public relations problem is a communication breakdown. One can very simply estimate the strength of this principle by examining textbooks on public relations to see how much space is given to the subject of communication. It is generally a lot. In the United States the first university courses in public relations were included in programmes of journalism, and the first public relations programmes were established in departments of mass communication. Its academic link with mass communication is still strong but more recently public relations has also found acceptance in departments of business administration.

Any human relationship can quite reasonably be thought of as an exercise in communication. But this does not simplify the concept; rather, it reveals its enormous complexity. The innumerable forms of communication that characterize a marriage, for example, and their subtlety, are a formidable challenge to anyone who sets about to study them. And the complexity of inter-group relationships is perhaps even more bewildering. Public relations is the management of all the relationships that exist between a complexity called an organization and all the individuals or other groups with which it interacts. It is therefore, by anybody's standards, a challenging profession.

Unfortunately in public relations practice communication often means nothing more than mass media communication. Thus the emphasis on media relations. This is undoubtedly a very important part of the job, but a good working relationship with the media does not necessarily mean effective communication with one's publics. People receive media messages in personal, social and cultural contexts that significantly affect their responses. A good practitioner appreciates this and makes it his business to understand the context of messages as well as their content and the media through which they are transmitted. This can draw him to look into matters he may never have thought relevant to public relations: sociology, political science, psychology, economics, semiotics, anthropology, to name but a few. He must use all the helpful resources available to him. To the degree that he limits his concern to media relations and his operational style to that of business administration, he inhibits his practice. He should be an intellectual, a person with a lively curiosity, a developed capacity for understanding and a respect for the full range and diversity of intellectual possibility.

The image of public relations

Public relations practitioners do not generally think of themselves as intellectuals, and they are not usually thought of as such. Which attitude engenders the other is debatable. In any case, it is a situation that seems to add weight to the arbitrary and damaging notion that public relations is the professional reserve of shallow extroverts who just like to meet people. The fact that few universities offer degrees in public relations reinforces this view. It is still not generally considered an independent intellectual pursuit. Consequently, if a practitioner has higher education it is usually in some other field. Bad enough that he inherits no tradition of scholarly discipline: the origins of his profession can in fact be traced to showmanship. Moreover, he is not allowed to forget that, in the language of the street, 'PR' is a verb: 'to PR' something means to cover up its defects and make it publicly attractive.

Nevertheless, whether it is generally realized or not there are many respectable intellectuals in public relations—people of depth and integrity who take time to ponder before they act and keep a very loose rein on their intelligence. Unfortunately they are often stereotyped as eccentrics by those who glory in the so-called urgencies of the practice.

REACTIVS:- DEALING WITH
PROBLEMS.

2. Situation Analysis

PROACTIVS:- ACCELERATING
GROWTH.

Reactive and Proactive Public Relations

The first stage in the public relations process, today commonly called 'Situation Analysis', was at one time called 'Problem Identification'. Before considering the different perspective suggested by the new term, a word about what the two points of view have in common.

Resources are never unlimited. There is always a limited number of people available to work on a public relations programme, limited facilities, materials, time and money. All of these must therefore be used wisely. More than one promising programme has ruefully starved to death before achieving its purpose. But even powerful organizations with enviable resources prefer a well directed lean-and-clean approach. In the jargon of the trade, 'efficiency' is the word. Efficiency, however, has its price: First one must fully grasp the situation. You cannot plan until you have set objectives, and you cannot set objectives until you see clearly what is wrong, what is right, and what could swing either way.

Situation analysis

It used to be that pre-planning research was undertaken only to detect problems, for which reason it was logically called 'Problem Identification'. If no problems were discovered, one seldom went further. In fact, it was thought dangerous to go further: 'Don't tamper with a winning combination' was the adage of the conventionally wise. Experience, however, has taught otherwise. Certainly if problems are uncovered they must be dealt with. This is termed Reactive Public Relations, or more bluntly Fire-Fighting Public Relations. But if research shows that all is going well, most organizations today take advantage of that grace period to look ahead, to foresee potential growth areas and the possible emergence of problems. They then refine their operation to assure continual development. This is termed Proacive Public

17

Relations and the pre-planning research it entails, Situation Analysis. Proactive and reactive policies are sometimes debated as though the choice between them were simply a matter of efficiency. Which policy will result in the more efficient deployment of resources? However, it could well be that the organization's survival, not merely efficiency, is in the balance.

Maintaining equilibrium

An organization guided entirely by a fire-fighting (reactive) policy functions in a pre-planned way until disturbed by a threatening situation when it responds defensively. Once the threat has been eliminated, the organization returns to its pre-planned way of life. This policy implies that the organization is in equilibrium; it is a steady-state system with no growth or evolution. If the equilibrium breaks down nothing can be said about the organization's future. A steady-state system is assumed to have the capacity to impose its will on the environment rather than give in to it. The environment may change but the organization will not; it endures. It is doubtful that there are any such organizations in the world, but many shortsightedly behave as if they were in equilibrium. Even if they were, however, they would benefit from proactive policies. If you can foresee problems, you can either avoid them altogether or at least reduce your vulnerability by preparing yourself for them.

More importantly though for most organizations, a total dependence on reactive policies inhibits a creative response to change. Organizations concerned about their development therefore need more sophisticated policies. What are the alternatives? To my knowledge no one has analysed them more lucidly than Karl W Deutsch in his book *The Nerves of Government* (New York, The Free Press of Glencoe, 1963). Although first published in 1963 it remains relevant. Deutsch considers four models of communication and control, one of which is the Equilibrium Model we have just discussed. The other three, called self-steering, are the Goal-Seeking Model, the Learning Model and the Consciousness Model.

Goal-seeking organizations

A goal-seeking organization is one whose principal goal is outside itself, unlike a steady-state system whose primary goal is its own stability. The goal-seeking organization responds to any input of information related to the pursuit of its goal—whether the information be threatening or positive. And it goes further: it includes the results of its own reaction in the new information by which it modifies its subsequent behaviour. In other words, it responds not only to the initial stimulus but also to feedback from its response. If its first response falls short of reaching the required adjustment, the action is continued; if it overshoots the mark it is reversed. A series of continuations and reversals might then take place resulting in a succession of diminishing mistakes gradually converging on the goal.

The proper functioning of a goal-seeking organization depends on the measurement of two factors — lag and gain. Lag is the time which elapses between the moment that positive or negative information is received and the moment necessary corrective action is taken. Gain is the extent of corrective action. The procedure might be compared to the reaction of a car driver who realizes he is heading for a kerb. Lag is the time which elapses between that realization and the moment he turns the steering wheel. Gain is the extent to which his turning of the wheel diverts him from the kerb. If he has not turned enough his corrective action must be continued; if he has turned too much he will find himself heading towards the opposite kerb and the corrective action will have to be reversed. An unskilled driver may go through a series of continuations and reversals until the car is once again on course. An organization which, because of its structure and operational style, cannot reduce the lag in its response sufficiently, must compensate for that by providing itself with some lead time. In other words, it must find a way to foresee problems and opportunities accurately from a greater distance. This is where proactive policies become essential.

Learning organizations

Goal-seeking organizations may have any number of goals, but once established they are assumed to be unchanging. There are, however, organizations whose goals are subject to continual change, for example, a social service agency which must respond to a sudden and unforeseen rise in local unemployment. Such organizations must have a capacity to reappraise their objectives, a willingness to change them if necessary, and the flexibility to reallocate their resources accordingly. Their ability to respond effectively to goal-changing circumstances depends largely on the number and kinds of their uncommitted resources (idle and reassignable resources) and on an adequate capacity for the storage and retrieval of information from their own past. In other words, they must have good memories. They must learn from experience, which is why they are called learning systems; and they must be able to apply what they have learned to the pursuit of changing goals, which is why they need proactive policies.

Conscious organizations

Conscious systems, like learning systems, respond both to external change affecting their pursuit of established goals, and to goal-modifying circumstances. But they respond also to their own internal changes which are caused by external factors. If the social service agency reacts to increased local unemployment by restructuring its organization, reassigning personnel and modifying its budget allocations, it must then monitor the internal effects of these changes (as well as the external ones, of course), compare the derived information to that stored in its memory and ensure that these internal feedbacks influence the agency's subsequent behaviour. Clearly, an effective response to internal change depends not only on monitoring and memory, but also on lag and gain; and the control of lag and gain depends on proactive policies.

Information requirements

A self-steering organization must therefore receive a steady flow of three kinds of information: information about its environment, information from its own past, and information about its present condition and the functioning of its parts. If this information flow is inadequate or if the organization does not use it well it risks serious losses, among them the following:

— The loss of power which would diminish its capacity to control a changing environment or to neutralize it—it would risk having to give in to circumstances;
— The loss of its capacity to receive information from outside, through a reduction in the effectiveness of its intake channels;
— The loss of its steering capacity, that is, of its ability to modify its behaviour with sufficient speed and precision;
— The loss of its capacity to recall and recombine information stored in its memory;
— The loss of its capacity to rearrange its structure or reallocate resources.

Any of these losses, and certainly any combination of them, could seriously jeopardize the organization's very survival. But by what logic is it said that their avoidance depends on a steady stream of information from within the system and from the world outside? Both experience and analysis reveal that all the aforementioned losses derive from an over-evaluation of the immediate over the long-term, the familiar over the new, the past over the present, the present over the future, the organization over its environment, commitments over new approaches, and present structures over fundamental reorganization. The defence against these weaknesses lies in a frank recognition of one's limitations and an openness to change. The first calls for self-awareness, the second for an awareness of what is going on in the world outside.

We have made no direct application of Deutsch's self-steering models to the field of public relations. But clearly, the policies of a public relations department or consultancy must be fully in line with the general operating policies of the client-organization. Therefore, to the degree that an organization benefits from proactive policies the pre-planning research undertaken by the public relations department must go beyond problem identification; it must, in the broadest sense of the term, be situation analysis.

Information gathering

At this point many textbooks suggest ways to gather information—desk research, field research, communications audits, customer surveys etc—all helpful, but the fundamental thing is that one must be guided always by the three types of information needed for proactive public relations:

(1) information about the organization's present structure, functions and resources;
(2) information about the organization's past;
(3) information about its environment.

The latter category includes information about the nature of the organization's publics, their dispositions, present forms of behaviour and the circumstances in which they live, work and relate to the organization.

Since gathering all this information can demand special research skills (as we will see later in this chapter), the question immediately arises: who should do it—an in-house team or an external consultancy? Many organizations are guided by the principle that *external public relations contracts are required only when the demands of a task go beyond the strengths and mix of in-house resources.* That is a respectable view; however, one should give special consideration to two implied criteria—objectivity and neutrality.

Objectivity

Objectivity relates to one's understanding of a situation. An objective understanding is based solidly on facts—all the facts; personal interpretation does not enter into it. Neutrality has to do with the judgements one makes on the basis of that understanding. An in-house team has the advantage of being already familiar with the organization's structure, functions and resources. What it does not already know should be readily available to it. An external consultancy would be starting from scratch. However, the in-house team could be led by its familiarity with the situation to overlook certain facts or make unwarranted assumptions. It is not a question of incorrectly interpreting facts, it is a matter of partial blindness. It can happen that they see the situation in terms of the organization's resources, defining problems according to the means available to solve them. Thus a conflict of interests might be seen as a 'communication problem' because the organization has effective channels of communication at its disposal; unemployment might be seen as a problem of 'cultural adjustment' because the organization is prepared to sponsor seminars on the cultural impact of new technologies. As a consequence of this impaired vision, the researchers' situation analysis would not be based on a complete inventory of facts. Needless to say, this does not always happen nor is it always clear that an external consultancy would be more objective, but it is something to be kept in mind.

The question of neutrality is more complicated since in this context it cannot be separated from the concepts of bias and advocacy.

Neutrality, Bias and Advocacy

A public relations practitioner (even when doing situation analysis) operates between an organization and its publics. He respects both parties. But is he neutral? Should he be? Can he be? To say he is neutral means he works for the best interests of both sides, favouring neither. To say (as is often said) that he is an advocate for the organization means that his loyalty is committed to one of the two parties. To say that he is biased implies that he makes decisions in favour of the organization. The neutral position is publicly acceptable; the advocacy position has at times to be defended because some people think it is unfair; a bias in favour of the organization may be thought unethical by those who oppose it. The truth is, the public relations practitioner is never neutral, he inevitably makes value and political judgements that favour the organization, and when he functions as an advocate it is to publicly defend or promote those partisan decisions. None of this is inherently unethical.

Neutrality

Let us clear up the notion of neutrality first. When one of the two parties is paying your salary you are not neutral, no matter how hard you might try to be. Furthermore, public relations practice is largely directed either to problem solving or to problem avoidance. But whose problems? A situation may be a problem to many people, but its public relations effects are an organization's problem. One of the practitioner's fundamental tasks, therefore, is to relieve the organization of problems and this orientation immediately compromises his neutrality. Even when at times he recommends organization policy change in favour of the public, he is striving to improve a relationship which will redound to the benefit of the organization.

Bias

Concern for the organization's problems also draws the practitioner, willy-nilly, to making value and political judgements in favour of his employer. To begin with, in identifying problems he is guided by definitions of what his employer considers 'good'. Probably the organization's continual growth is considered good. Its participation in the life of the community is also probably defined as good. On a more general level, the continuing progress of established institutions is likely considered good. There are many more such defined maxims and collectively they serve as primary moral principles of organization value judgements. Problems are then defined as threats to these accepted maxims. In other words, a 'problem' is formulated out of the troubles that *administrators* believe they face. The practitioner engaged in identifying public relations problems is therefore occupied in making value judgements which conform to the stance of his employer. Conversely, 'growth opportunities' are defined as situations which contribute to what the employer considers good. And the practitioner's pursuit of these opportunities reflects value judgements favouring his employer.

If a number of problems or opportunities are identified in situation analysis, their priorities are established by the same principles. At this point, however, value judgements often translate into political judgements. For example, a university might give high priority to the direct broadcast of televised courses to commercial firms in the community. Although spoken of as a public service to be provided by a community-minded institution, the underlying motive for the decision might very well be political: faced with the possibility of cuts in government education grants, the university may be trying to win the support of the business community in resisting the government's proposed policy. In a situation like this, the interaction of value and political principles draws the public relations practitioner to making judgements on both levels, and in each case he will respect his commitment to the good of his employer.

Assume for the moment that the university's proposed project is resisted by faculty members required to give the televised courses. The practitioner is now faced with an additional public relations problem—this time between the university Management and the faculty. Conceivably the situation might now be described in different terms. The offering of televised courses might be called a creative application of progressive technology. And it may be suggested that faculty members who oppose it are suffering from culture lag. 'Progressive technology', 'culture lag', are value-laden terms. They express the value judgements of Management. But the practitioner who uses them reflects not only a moral choice in favour of his employer but a political siding as well: he is on the side of power holders in a conflict with subordinates.

The search for mutual understanding

Typically, many value and political judgements shape the nature and objectives of a public relations project. These preliminary judgements form part of the process of disentangling facts, half-truths, obvious choices, misconceptions, hopes and desired goals—in other words, the search for mutual understanding between the organization and its various publics. The hope is that in the situation analysis a harmony of interests will be discovered. But what if this does not happen? What if it becomes evident that there exists a genuine conflict of values between them? In the example of the university proposing to offer televised courses, the new value (a direct involvement with the business community) cannot be accepted without sacrificing an old value (academic detachment). Which is to be preferred? An innocent public relations practitioner might cling to the hope of eventually making everybody happy (as though that were the ultimate criterion by which his work is to be judged). But a more experienced and realistic one will again find himself siding with his employer, in other words supporting the established power.

What C Wright Mills said in 1959 still applies: 'Nowadays attempts to make...specific policies palatable, are often very much a part of "personnel administration" and "public relations".' (Wright Mills, 1959, p.93)

Power

Unless Management's position is blatantly unacceptable, it is not surprising that the public relations practitioner endorses it: he is not neutral, he works for Management. Undoubtedly therefore, he will also share with Management the difficult task of winning general acceptance of the final decision. No matter how it is expressed, the enforcement of a decision is always an exercise of power. Power is the capability to exercise one's will over that of others and over the environment. It means not having to give in. When they implement their value judgements over opposition the established authorities are exercising power, and the public relations practitioner inevitably participates in the exercise. The means by which he and Management do this may vary from one situation to another but almost certainly they will begin by trying to make their position intelligible. If they succeed and if that is enough to make it acceptable, fine. If not, a process of persuasion must follow. Logical analysis, emotive eloquence, possibly implied warnings of dire consequences should the project decision not be supported, may be issued. But for all that, one cannot eliminate the possibility that some form of coercion will finally be required. This is an extremely difficult aspect of public relations which any practitioner would prefer to avoid. But if coercion becomes necessary, the practitioner will be involved—precisely because of his commitment to his employer. The very possibility that this can occur flows from his non-neutrality, from his moral and political support for his employer.

A very important point: we are not talking here about blind support. It is not a question of bolstering a power that has lost its legitimacy. A public relations practitioner who spends his time trying to make emasculated power appear providential, or the frustrated powerless recognize the 'wisdom' of their leaders, is contemptible. What is at issue here is an altogether different kind of moral confrontation. Conflicts are not always between people who are right and others who are wrong. They are more often between opponents who both hold acceptable views, but views which in practice are irreconcilable. In such a case, a solution has to be imposed. If the power that imposes it is legitimate, operating within the limits of its authority, this is a perfectly acceptable practice. And it is not to the discredit of public relations that it should participate in the exercise of that power.

The advocacy role

Both non-neutrality and bias (in the strict sense in which we have used the term), although justifiable, admittedly have negative connotations. Practitioners therefore prefer to call themselves, more positively, advocates for their clients. It is an accepted public relations principle that *the public relations practitioner supports his client as much as possible and continually tries to promote his best interests*. This is advocacy. If accused of covering over his client's weaknesses with silence, the practitioner rebuts that he is no more bound to divulge them than a defence lawyer is expected to speak ill of his clients. If there are grounds for suspecting that the practitioner is being less than candid, it is considered the role of a consumer's advocate to represent the public in an inquiry.

Clearly there is nothing inherently wrong in promoting an organization's best interests and taking no active part in publicizing its weaknesses. However, practitioners do themselves a disservice when they compare their practice to that of legal advocates. The two advocacy roles are exercised in totally different circumstances. First, while there are such things as ombudsmen and offices willing to act on behalf of consumers, most publics are not represented by them in less-than-spectacular dealings with organizations. If the public is represented by an unofficial spokesman, there are no established rules and procedures governing the debate as there are in the case of legal trials. And finally, no independent magistrate is appointed to pass final judgement. The notion that the 'court of public opinion' will ultimately decide is a meaningless platitude. In respectable public relations practice there is no need of a court; in malpractice, public opinion is not the court but the plaintiff.

Return now to the principle of choosing an external agency only when the demands of a task surpass the strengths and mix of in-house resources. Since the in-house practitioner is not neutral but exercises an advocacy role for his client, there might well be times when an external agency would be preferable regardless of the quality of in-house resources—especially for situation analysis which demands objectivity and impartial judgement. It must be emphasized, though, that an external agency's objectivity, competence and reliability should not be taken for granted.

Research Methods

In discussing proactive public relations, the point was made that self-steering organizations need steady inputs of information about themselves and their external world. This feedback amounts to continuous situation analysis. If it is continuous and systematic it will periodically point to opportunities or problems which call for more careful study. Such periodic studies, although included as elements of pre-planning research, are projects in their own right and must be guided by clearly defined objectives. However, to say that research objectives must be clearly defined is not to say that the problem or opportunity of interest is yet clearly understood. Consider, for example, a municipal housing authority which becomes aware of some rumbling discontent in a low-income housing estate. The problem at this stage is still unclear, but the objectives of a research project would be very precise—to discover the exact nature and roots of the discontent. Since there is no fixed method for tackling problems, one must go about it in whatever way seems reasonable. Possibly in this case one might envisage a two-step process, the first being a broad-ranging study and the second a very sharply focused inquiry.

In the first stage the research team would examine all the background documentation on the housing estate in question and similar reports on comparable estates. They would interview experts on housing, on low-income populations and on any other aspect of the problem. Some residents of the estate would of course, also be interviewed, as would other people with relevant knowledge, for example local clergy, school teachers, health workers, police etc. The research team would also visit the estate to study its condition, design and anything else of interest. Let us assume that this wide-ranging study strongly suggested that the discontent derived from interracial occupancy. Tenants had been assigned flats by the housing authority without any consideration of race, and the impact of that policy was now being felt. If the research team were sufficiently sure of their tentative diagnoses, they would make it the focus of their second-step inquiry.

In the second stage the approach would be more systematic. Since the problem of interest is socio-cultural, the team would probably use sociological research methods to discover the residents' attitudes. This would almost certainly entail selecting a sample of tenants to be questioned, designing a questionnaire, administering it, processing the results and determining their significance. Each of these details must be handled with unquestionable competence if the validity of the survey is to be assured. It should therefore be (but unfortunately is not) an inviolable principle that *in public relations, sociological surveys, are carried out only by properly trained people.*

The practitioner's role in research

Most public relations practitioners are not trained in research methods and yet the need for sociological research, especially attitude surveys, frequently arises in their work. When that happens, therefore, the wisest choice is to contract the work out. This does not mean, however, that the public relations practitioner should be barred from the process as if he were a contaminating agent. An organization's public relations officer should be familiar enough with the basics of sociological research methods to be able to appreciate what is being done, to assess its quality and perhaps contribute to it in a limited way. His views should weigh heavily, for example, on the selection of an appropriate level of analysis for the research. The choice is not always as obvious as in the example we have just considered. Some problems are best researched on a national level, more insight can be gained on others if they are studied in a housing estate, a local authority area, a rural community or church diocese. One must select a unit in which the problem exists in its full complexity and where its elements are clearly observable, and this is something the in-house public relations officer might know better than an outsider could.

The level of analysis will then determine the nature and size of the sample to be studied. The public relations officer should understand the differences between probability and non-probability samples, simple and stratified random samples and cluster samples. And he should appreciate the suitability or non-suitability of each type to his problem. He should understand that the inferences he will later be able to draw from the research findings will depend considerably on the size of the sample. An impressively designed survey can be rendered invalid because of an inadequate number of respondents. In designing the questionnaire the researchers may structure the questions in such a way that the number of possible responses is limited, for example, 'strongly agree—agree—disagree—strongly disagree'. The public relations officer should understand the reasons for doing this and the special advantages and limitations of each available method. Also, he should respect the researchers' phrasing of the questions which may at times be subtle but is always very important. The pros and cons of the various ways of administering a questionnaire (mail, telephone, door-to-door etc) should interest the public relations officer not only from cost considerations but also by reason of their diverse effects on the quality of responses. While the mechanical processing of the data need not especially interest him, the selection of appropriate analytical computer programs should, since this bears directly on the interpretation of the findings.

In this final stage—the interpretation of results—the public relations officer resumes his full function as director of the situation analysis and it is important that he does so. The research team will generally submit with their findings, a calculation of their 'statistical significance'. This concerns the likelihood that the observed survey results might be explained by pure chance. The calculation will place that likelihood somewhere between 0 and 100 per cent. But at what level should it be considered 'significant'? The researchers will set an arbitrary level—say, one occurrence out of 100 observations—and this they will call the 'level of significance'. If the survey findings go beyond that level one is advised to be concerned, below it one can be 'statistically' indifferent. It is unfortunate that this calculation is referred to as a standard of 'significance'. It is nothing more than a statistical point of reference. It has no essential significance and should never be taken as a *necessarily* weighty factor in public relations planning. The true significance of statistical findings can be perceived only when they are considered in their full context. Cultural factors might bear on their appraisal, as might historical circumstances, economic conditions etc, all of which must, therefore, enter into situation analysis. It is the public relations officer's responsibility to see that they do.

Opinion Leaders

The kind of research just described can take months to carry out and can cost a lot. Not surprisingly therefore, public relations departments which either cannot afford the money or prefer not to spend the time look for other ways to achieve the same results: there aren't any. As a second-best approach, however, one can sometimes obtain helpful information from someone who has already done a survey. To be unquestionably helpful such second-hand information must satisfy two criteria:

(1) It must have been obtained from a survey of the public in question or of one comparable to it in all of its pertinent characteristics;
(2) The purpose of the previous survey must have been such that no unreasonable assumptions are needed to apply its findings to the problem under study.

The public relations practitioner must decide for himself whether assumptions are 'unreasonable' and whether the two publics are 'comparable' on all 'pertinent' characteristics. In any case, one must always be extremely careful in drawing inferences from secondhand surveys.

As a third option some practitioners operate on a principle that is ill-founded and very dangerous. They assume that the opinions of journalists and 'opinion leaders' can provide a reasonable estimate of public opinion. And since these sources can be consulted at less cost than it would take to conduct a survey, they think it is a more economical approach. It may well be cheaper but, unfortunately, there is no assurance of its validity. Those who advocate this 'economical' option do not usually define what they mean by 'opinion leaders', but since they so often speak of journalists in the same breath, one might infer that they think opinion leaders are simply people in touch with enough other people to know what the whole population thinks, and they erroneously assume that journalists are that much in touch. A lot of journalists just as naively and erroneously believe that taxi drivers are opinion leaders of that kind. It is worth mentioning that when newspaper editors want to know public opinion on an issue they almost always poll a sample of the population rather than simply ask the views of journalists.

To those who propose that instead of spending a lot of money on a public opinion survey, you can get a quick, cheap and valid reading of public opinion simply by asking opinion leaders what the public thinks, it must be emphasized here that this is a naive and dangerous view.

Research on opinion leadership

Over the past 40 years, opinion leadership has received a lot of attention in communication research. In the literature based on that research, an opinion leader is taken to be someone who, in the particular public in which he functions as such, contributes significantly to the formation of public opinion. Notice, it is not assumed that he shares the prevalent views of the public. He might share them; but on the other hand he might disagree with them emphatically, in which case he may try to exercise his leadership to change them. It could be, however, that he does not even realize he is an opinion leader. It is not a function attached to certain recognized occupations, for example that of a teacher, a social worker or a journalist. Opinion leaders are often unobtrusively influential. This is why it is difficult to identify them. Sometimes they are respected because they are so much like other members of the public; sometimes it is because they are attractively different. Sometimes they have deep genealogical and cultural roots in the community; sometimes they are relative outsiders who bring new information and fresh perspectives. Sometimes they are prominent public figures; sometimes they are elusive loners. In any case they are always limited in the scope and territorial extent of their influence. In other words, none of them is an opinion leader everywhere on everything. One whose political views are respected may have no influence whatsoever in matters of education, and a powerful moulder of opinion in his own community might be unknown or ignored in a neighbouring town. The single positive trait opinion leaders generally have in common is empathy — a disposition that enables them to appreciate the other person's point of view. A characteristic obviously not peculiar to members of special professions or to those of a particular social or cultural bent.

In the early 1950s the notion of opinion leadership was studied as an alternative to the view that the mass media directly shape public opinion. In the old view, the general public, the mass, was seen as a huge collection of individuals each one reacting irresistably to the messages of the media. The media were described as operating like hypodermic needles on their audiences. Once the message was injected, it was thought that the recipient could do little or nothing to resist its persuasive influence. Then around 1955 research seemed to indicate that people are more likely to be influenced by certain community leaders in forming their opinions, the opinion leaders themselves being directly influenced by the media. This became known as the 'Two-Step Flow' hypothesis and it certainly placed journalists and opinion leaders high in the ranks of those who shaped public views. But gradually the idea of a two-step flow came to be seen as an oversimplification, even a distortion, of the complicated process by which information is diffused and public opinion formed. The drift from that point was in two directions: some researchers returned to the belief that most people are directly influenced by the media; others favoured the view that there can be any number of intermediaries between the media and the public. The current view seems to be that anything can happen: people can be directly influenced by the media, or they can get their information and opinions from one, two or any number of intermediaries.

Because opinion leaders were originally thought to influence the formation of public opinion, they came at the same time to be thought of as people who could tell you what public opinion is. It is in this capacity that they are, even today, consulted by the credulous who want a quick and inexpensive reading of public opinion. But articulating public opinion is entirely different from influencing its formation. There is no reason to assume that the two functions are always performed by the same people. Who then does reliably express public opinion? It is impossible to give a satisfactory answer. Such people can vary enormously from one public to another, and they can be very hard for an outsider to track down. Certainly there is no basis for the assumption that members of certain professions, for example, journalists, act in that capacity.

In the responsible practice of public relations, the following principle applies: *To determine the opinion of a given public on a specific question, either a survey is commissioned or reference is made to a reliable and relevant one that has already been carried out.*

3. Final Objectives

Parameters of Public Relations Objectives

In situation analysis anything observed working against what Management defines as 'good' is considered to be a 'problem', anything that advances Management's declared aims is seen as an 'opportunity'. Perhaps the simplest and most fundamental of Management's aims is public acceptance of the organization. Stronger sentiments like respect, appreciation or pride are always of course welcome, and Management understandably hopes that all public attitudes will translate into things like purchase of goods or services, the support of a cause or endorsement of an ideology; but public acceptance is the base.

Public acceptance depends very much on public perception. We respect organizations we perceive as respectable; we support organizations we perceive as deserving support. We may sometimes avail ourselves of the goods or services of organizations we dislike (for example, we may complain about the quality of public transport but still take the bus to work), but that generally happens only when we are compelled by necessity. As a rule, an organization's public acceptance depends on how the public perceives it. What is more, public perception can depend on the organization's efforts to make itself known and understood. Therefore, the objectives of any public relations project or programme are ultimately means by which Management hopes to enhance public perception of the organization by making it better known and understood. (An exception to this may seem to be pre-planning research which consists more of receiving information than of spreading it, but it is merely preliminary to the dissemination.) Self-revelation, however, implies self-knowledge which in this case implies that the public relations practitioner know his organization thoroughly. It is important to understand what that means.

The corporate portrait

We speak about an organization as 'honest', 'reliable', 'dedicated

33

to progress', etc as though these were stable characteristics, qualities making up what might be called its corporate personality. (By personality I mean the ensemble of inherited and acquired characteristics that make a person unique.) But an organization is not a person, it does not have a true personality; it has no psychic centre in which traits like 'honesty' or 'fidelity' are inherent. An organization is an assembly of human beings, each of them with an individual personality, but the organization does not have one of its own. The organization does have patterns of behaviour which may be reliable, but these reflect Management decisions not stable dispositions of the organization itself.

In other words, to the degree that we attribute personality traits to an organization we are in the realm of fiction — a helpful fiction, but fiction nonetheless. We act *as if* the organization had a personality of its own. The public relations practitioner who has to get to know the organization searches its history, studies its objectives and observes its interaction with its environment as if to discover its inherent qualities. The result, however, is not the discovery of a corporate personality but that of a corporate portrait. It is the portrait that Management wants to present to the public. The Management team might not think of it as a portrait; to them it may be simply the ensemble of objectives, policies, procedures and performance that defines the organization. But it is a portrait nonetheless. Furthermore, because it is a portrait of something that has no objective existence, it is necessarily an agreed-upon perception. It is agreed upon by Management and entrusted to the public relations practitioner for public dissemination.

To display the full portrait all at once would be a bit much: it contains too much information for the public to assimilate. Generally therefore, it is revealed through a series of images, each one partial, each selected to meet a public or corporate need. For example, at a certain time it might be important to show the organization's concern for the environment; at another time a creative response to public disorder or a clarification of policy or a broadening of its application, might be called for. An annual report is a partial image, so is an open house or a television interview. In short, any public relations project is the public presentation of an element of the corporate portrait agreed upon by Management. And this basic purpose is reflected in the project's objectives.

Mutual understanding

Described in this way, public relations appears to be a one-way communication, yet those who speak for the profession insist that it is two-way. It is spoken of as a dialogue between an organization and its publics, a pursuit of mutual understanding. This perception is in fact embodied in one of the most basic of all public relations principles: *Public relations seeks to establish and maintain mutual understanding between an organization and its publics.* Mutual understanding means that each of two parties understands the other — in this case, the organization and each of its publics. Having discussed the difficulties the organization encounters in this task, consider now those faced by its publics.

A public, like an organization, has no personality of its own (the single exception being a public consisting of one person). It is a community of people each one of whom has a unique personality which cannot be shared. Unlike an organization, however, a public may not have an agreed-upon perception of itself. A relatively small and homogeneous public like an association of dog breeders might know itself quite well, but a meandering city suburb may not even be aware of its own membership. Nor is any member of a public necessarily responsible for the composition of a self-portrait or for its presentation to others. By default, therefore, an organization that wants to understand a public usually has to take the initiative. It must do what it can to get to know that public. However, since the public does not have an objectively real personality the organization must compose a portrait of it based on what it can determine about the beliefs, attitudes, opinions and behaviour of its members. The resulting image is necessarily limited and poorly defined; also, it represents nothing more than a moment in the life of an ever-changing reality; but it is the best one can do.

Organization objectives

Given the constraints on the organization and those on the public, complete mutual understanding between them has to be considered an impossible dream. Still, the principle that public relations 'seeks' to establish and maintain it is commendable: it defines the home territory of the profession and offers guidance to practitioners in setting objectives. Nevertheless it must be admitted that, as a guiding principle, the pursuit of mutual understanding is somewhat idealistic. The practitioner needs more practical directives as well. The following imperative, taken from a standard public relations textbook, is generally accepted as a practical principle: '*Public relations goals clearly and absolutely contribute to overall organization objectives.*' There can be no doubt about the necessity expressed in this principle nor about its direct bearing on the setting of project objectives. However, an analysis of it reveals ambiguities and leads us on to some cogent principles.

First, it is said that public relations must contribute to 'overall' organization objectives. Does that mean 'all' of the organization's objectives, or the 'main' ones, or any selection from the full list which would constitute a reasonable workload? If it means all of the organization's objectives then it includes the main ones, so let us consider that possibility first—that public relations must contribute to the main objectives of the organization. In the case of a car manufacturer could that mean anything other than that public relations must contribute to the sale of cars? Interpreted in this way the principle would mean that the company must sell more cars with public relations than without it. No matter what variety of functions the public relations department may perform (pursuit of mutual understanding, public information, crisis management etc) and no matter how indirect their relationship to the organization's main objective, if in the end more cars are not sold then by this interpretation of the principle public relations has failed. In commercial organizations, therefore, the principle would link public relations firmly to the sales of goods and services, because that is their main objective. Public relations would thus become confused with marketing, advertising, publicity and promotion. In non-commercial organizations the same reasoning would lead to the conclusion that public relations must result in an increase of services utilized, votes tallied, recruits enlisted, donations received, etc.

The contribution of public relations

How can one know whether public relations has made such a contribution? It must be demonstrated by either logic or measurement. For example, since most people would not buy a car from a company they suspect of dishonesty, it could be logically argued that a public relations programme designed to enhance the organization's public image would contribute to car sales. But situations are not always that clear-cut. If a company has for years been publicly accepted, could it not just as logically be argued that the dependable quality of its cars alone is enough to sustain sales, and that this traditional quality is brought to public attention through advertising, marketing and publicity? Why continue to have a public relations department? If a sudden problem arises, one can always bring in a consultant on contract. In many situations, therefore, the more convincing justification for continuing public relations is a measurable contribution to organization objectives. But this is not easily obtained. Consider again the case of the car manufacturer.

Clearly a number of factors contribute to the sale of the product—the principal ones for our purposes being marketing, advertising, publicity and public relations. These are generally considered to be discrete functions but in practice they overlap notoriously. Their individual causal influence on the sale of cars cannot, therefore, be isolated and measured separately. They form a single multivariate influence whose components are only vaguely distinguishable. And if you cannot separate the causes you cannot isolate their individual effects. In other words, there is no way of measuring public relations' unique contribution to the sale of cars. The same could be said of its contribution to the main goals of a commercial service organization, or of any organization in which its effects cannot be separately measured. In organizations where the public relations department operates alone, that is, where there are no departments of marketing, advertising, publicity, etc, the situation may be different. But if the public relations department exercises all the functions that would normally be performed by separate departments, then there is really no difference. The effects of the public relations function would be inseparable from those of the others.

Secondary goals

There is no convincing proof, therefore, either by logic or measurement, that public relations always contributes to the main objectives of most organizations. One suspects that it does, but there is no solid proof. The possibility remains, however, that it makes a consistent and demonstrable contribution to some secondary goals—goals unrelated to marketing, advertising, etc, goals which public relations alone can attain. For example, a manufacturing company may include among its goals that of making a positive contribution to the life of the community in which its plant is located. This can be pure public relations and the effects of any effort to achieve the goals might be discernible. One could argue that in the long run such a secondary goal would contribute to the sale of products; possibly. But even if that did not happen, the public relations effort would be justified as contributing to an established organization goal, albeit not the main one. If it could be shown that it also contributed to the sale of products, so much the better. The situation would be intolerable only if public relations, in pursuing its proper objectives, inhibited the attainment of the organization's main goals.

Therefore, in preference to the single principle quoted earlier, the following two principles are submitted:

(1) *Public relations objectives never impede the attainment of any more important organization objectives;*
(2) *Public relations contributes demonstrably to the attainment of any one or more of the organization's objectives.*

Fixed, Flexible, Feasible and Measurable Goals

Public relations objectives are determined only partly by the nature of the problems or opportunities to which they are directed. Two other important factors are:

(1) The nature of the organization, which includes its objectives and the mentality of its Management;
(2) Feasibility.

The nature of the organization

Consider first the nature of the organization. The final objectives of a public relations project have to be considered in their place in a gamut of possible objectives—intermediate project objectives, final project objectives, intermediate organization objectives and final organization objectives. Causal influences move from one end of this chain to the other. Thus, the attainment of intermediate project objectives leads to the attainment of final project objectives. Final project objectives lead, in their turn, to the attainment of organization objectives. But shaping influences move in the opposite direction: the nature of organization objectives shapes that of project objectives. Therefore, the final project objectives we are now considering are shaped not only by the problems or opportunities to which they are directed, but also by the organization's objectives.

If the organization has a fixed final objective, for example the promotion of animal rights, its operational style may have to be quite flexible to adapt to environmental change without losing its essential direction. Its intermediate objectives might therefore change frequently. Since these intermediate objectives influence public relations project objectives, such an organization might need an innovative public relations department with a capacity for setting flexible project objectives.

The effect on public relations project objectives is likely to be the same in the case of an organization with changing final objectives. In that case the organization's intermediate objectives and consequently its public relations project objectives would have to change accordingly.

Management mentality

Is there any situation then in which public relations project objectives would be relatively stable? Indeed yes: imagine an organization intent on establishing itself as an unchanging national institution. This objective might well reflect a conservative Management keen on projecting a corporate image of traditionalism or cultural purity. The mentality of its Management might be such that the public relations department has limited scope in selecting project objectives. Remember that every project objective is the projection of a partial image of the corporate portrait agreed upon by Management. A rigidly conservative Management limits itself to a certain number of problem solutions. If there are four conceivable solutions to a problem the department might find itself restricted to two which meet with Management approval. And once set, these objectives are relatively stable: conservatism and stability complement each other. In extreme cases all problems may be 'solved' by some application of fascism. The closer an organization gets to that state the less need it may have for a public relations department, but many organizations while yet distanced from fascism impose a rigid conservatism on their public relations departments. How much innovative freedom, for example, would the public relations departments of certain fundamentalist religious sects have in setting project objectives? While the stability of the Church's purpose might suggest a public relations approach flexible enough to steer through ever-changing circumstances without losing its fix on the final goal, the mentality of its Management limits it to a narrow range of options. In effect, the public relations department loses its self-steering capacity and approaches the equilibrium condition described by Deutsch.

Open-minded management is therefore a necessary condition for the setting of flexible public relations project goals, that is, goals which may be modified during the project. Self-steering systems will probably find that flexible project objectives are necessary for the attainment of changing organization goals. But in equilibrium systems with fixed final goals the nature and stability of project objectives may depend almost entirely on Management mentality. In this case, at the project level the choice between fixed and flexible objectives is never purely tactical.

Feasibility

The setting of project objectives is also constrained by feasibility. It makes no sense to set goals that cannot be reached. When one thinks of feasibility one thinks immediately of resources—time, personnel, facilities, materials and money. An organization's resources are never unlimited, but precisely what portion of them is allocated to a given project (thus limiting feasible options) depends on the priority assigned to the project. And here, as in the establishment of project objectives, Management mentality may exercise a stronger influence than the nature of the problem or opportunity to which the project is directed. Creative projects may be resisted by conservative Management. Whether this is ultimately good or bad depends on the degree to which the organization's self-steering capacity is thereby put at risk. Deutsch (1963, Chapter 2) warns that this risk is aggravated by an over-evaluation of the immediate over the long-term, the familiar over the new, the organization over its environment, commitments over new approaches and present structure over fundamental reorganization. At times, therefore, it falls to the public relations department to convince Management that a project's priority be reappraised in light of the organization's need to maintain its self-steering power. An over-concern for here-and-now feasibility can lead to a preference for acceptable project results over ideal ones.

Measurability

A further consideration in setting objectives is the degree to which project results must be measurable. A reasonable estimate of success or failure might at times be enough but frequently greater precision is necessary. In evaluation, whether of end results or of progress during project implementation, one measures against objectives and obviously the task is easier if the objectives are precisely measurable. If you hope for a 10 per cent increase in association membership over a year, at the end of the year you will know exactly how close you came to your objective. And during the year, the month-to-month enrolment figures may give you cause for either elation or discouragement. Not surprisingly then, public relations practitioners are generally advised to set precisely measurable project objectives, ideally quantitative ones. Unfortunately this is not always possible. For example, the pursuit of mutual understanding—a fundamental public relations objective—is not quantifiable; nor are beliefs, attitudes or sentiments. But the importance of these things to public relations inclines many practitioners to impose on them measurement scales that allow them to be analysed as if they were quantitative. Thus, although 'satisfaction' cannot be measured in discrete units, respondents are sometimes asked whether they are 'very dissatisfied, dissatisfied, satisfied or very satisfied' about something. And their responses are then treated as if they were precise measurements of 'satisfaction'. Does it make sense to do this?

Measurement scales

Suppose a practitioner is interested in studying attitudes towards his organization. If he simply wants to say whether two people differ in their attitudes, without saying how great the difference between them is or whether one is more favourable than the other, he must at least be able to distinguish different attitudes. If he cannot, he will never be able to say whether those of two people are the same or different. He may, however, want to go further. He may want to discover whether one person's attitude is more favourable than the other's (without specifying how much more favourable). In that case he will need a measurement technique that ranks them according to the intensity of their dispositions. Going further still, he may want to compare the differences between various pairs of people. Is the difference between A and B the same as that between C and D? In this case he must be able to measure precisely, and in equal units of measurement, the intervals between individuals. Finally, he may be interested in the ratios between attitudinal differences: 'Is X twice as favourable as Y towards our organization?' To know this, he will need an absolute zero point from which to measure (in equal units) each one's attitude. Corresponding to these four research interests, are four different measurement scales — nominal, ordinal, interval and ratio.

Nominal scales
A nominal scale measures only the equivalence or non-equivalence of two things. It will tell you whether they are alike or different. If appropriately structured it could be applied to a group of people to distinguish children from adults, but it would tell you nothing else.

Ordinal scales
An ordinal scale will tell you the relative positions of various subjects with respect to a certain characteristic. It will tell you whether A's attitude towards your organization is more favourable than B's, less favourable or equal to it. But if their attitudes

differ the scale won't measure the difference between them. For example, an employer might rank order job applicants by this scale—first choice, second choice, third choice etc—without indicating the distances between them as candidates.

Interval scales
An interval scale will not only rank order items but will also indicate the distances between them in units of equal measurement. You will thus be able to tell (a) precisely how much difference exists between any two of them; (b) whether two differences are equal; (c) if they are not equal, by how much one is greater than the other. A thermometer is an interval scale. Its markings indicate equal amounts of change in the volume of mercury under changing temperature. A change from 5 degrees to 10 degrees is the same as a change from 35 degrees to 40 degrees because in each case the temperatures are separated by five units and all units on the scale are equal.

Ratio scales
A ratio scale improves on an interval scale by measuring from an absolute zero. (A thermometer measures from an arbitrary zero: 0 degrees does not mean there is no temperature.) Because it measures from an absolute zero, this scale will tell you the ratio between two measured differences. It will tell you that the distance between A and B is twice as much (or half as much, 20 times as much etc) as that between G and H. All types of statistical analysis can be applied to data obtained from interval scales.

Measuring attitudes

It would be a great advantage in public relations if attitudes could be measured by ratio scales. We would be able to say, for example, that this campaign had twice the effect of last year's because public attitudes improved by twice as much. But does 'very satisfied' indicate twice as much satisfaction as merely 'satisfied'? Obviously it does not. Could the differences in satisfaction be measured on an interval scale? In other words, is the difference between 'satisfied' and 'very satisfied' the same as that between 'dissatisfied' and 'very dissatisfied'? There is no way of knowing. In measuring attitudes, the best we can generally do is to apply an ordinal scale that will tell us whether one attitude is more or less favourable than another, without telling us by how much.

Nevertheless, researchers frequently do analyse survey results as if they were interval data. They have no reasonable certainty that ranked responses are separated by equal units of measurement (as they must be to use this scale) but they are willing to assume that they are. They base their assumption on the judgements of large numbers of people. In other words, if a reasonably large number of selected judges have agreed that the distance between 'satisfied' and 'very satisfied' should be considered the same as that between 'dissatisfied' and 'very dissatisfied' then the researchers accept that as adequate foundation for their assumption. This has now become such common practice that project designers often set objectives which are not actually quantitative but which they are willing to treat as if they were. Thus, an objective to 'assess public response' to an organization's initiative is considered appropriate on the assumption that attitudinal responses can be validly measured on an interval scale. It must be said therefore that in public relations the oft-repeated rule that project objectives should be measurable is sometimes applied with questionable validity.

Objectives that Cannot be Measured

Precise and quantitative objectives are preferred in public relations because they allow criteria to be established for later evaluation of results. But the criteria for measuring results should be determined by the nature of objectives and not vice-versa. Practitioners can get so distracted by quantitative approaches, they overlook important qualitative objectives. For example, it is this author's view that an over-concern for measurable results explains the almost total neglect of public relations' social impact. It is a subject never mentioned in textbooks. Yet it could be stated as a principle: *public relations contributes inevitably to the socio-cultural environment in which it operates*. Admittedly it is not possible to measure this achievement but it deserves attention.

Social impact of public relations

To say that this contribution of public relations is inevitable is to say nothing of its quality or intensity. Whether it is good or bad, strong or weak, still depends on the practice. But if public relations abdicates responsibility for its contribution to social and cultural life it will, as a profession, lose control of its own future. The control of its inevitable contribution calls for a planned approach well set in an historical context.

In the 1960s, books on public relations frequently referred to the 'marketplace of ideas'—a hypothetical bazaar where public opinion was said to emerge from the free exchange of privately owned points of view. The marketplace still exists but it has changed. The stakes are higher now and bargaining is more restricted. What is negotiated now is the whole range of social and cultural values, the very definition of what is legitimate, required, peripheral or irrelevant—fashion, lifestyles, politics, books to be read, films to be seen, music to be listened to. Social competence is defined there and those whose social position depends on their competence go to the marketplace to find out what is required of them, what relationships they must cultivate to 'succeed'. Haggling in the new marketplace is not as open as it was in the old; participation is limited to those with power to influence (if not impose) the agenda and set the terms of debate.

The middle class

Jean-Paul Sartre's distinction is helpful here: the ends of society are defined, he says, by the dominant class and realized by the working class; but the means to the ends are reserved to an ensemble of technicians who belong to the third sector (Sartre, 1972, p.381). These technicians, as he calls them, control the new marketplace of ideas. They are middle-class people, experts in organization and communication. Among them one finds businessmen, journalists, medical practitioners, artists, university professors, clergymen, and others of equal social rank, but no manual labourers and no independently wealthy people. These people control public debate by controlling the media of communication. One should not think only of the press, radio and television as communications media. There are many others: schools, churches, department stores, rock concerts, cinema, sporting events, hotels and fashion shows. Any vehicle for public communication is a mass medium. Those who address the public through these media exercise an uncommon social influence and express a particular set of values. They are frequently seen, for example, on television chat shows: novelists, economists, psychologists, actors, discussing a whole range of social and cultural questions. Clergymen discuss the economy, painters comment on social ethics, historians express their views on alienation, psychologists reflect on consumerism. These chat show guests are not randomly selected; they are invited, and they accept, because they share the values reflected in the programme's agenda. In other words, collectively these people set the agenda and the terms for public discussion. This is a significant form of power.

Agenda setting

To illustrate how it works, consider an adage which found public acceptance long ago: 'Crime does not pay.' To set the question of illegal behaviour in those terms is to endorse and broaden the application of a highly questionable ethical norm—whatever does not pay is unacceptable. Crime is socially unacceptable because it does not pay. The promulgation of an arbitrary point of view has thus been managed by those who set the terms for discussion.

Another example: A motor insurance company opposing the proposed legalization of marijuana in Canada argued that legalizing the drug would increase its use and lead to more widespread consumption of harder drugs. The combination would certainly increase the number of traffic accidents and as a result insurance premiums would have to be raised. Consequently everyone would lose. That is, everyone would lose money. The proposed legislation was reduced to a financial threat.

Although these examples are of minor import, the pervasive and carefully orchestrated repetition of value messages year-in and year-out can have more significant consequences. Given the communication expertise of those who today control the market-place of ideas, they are able to influence many public values including those which ultimately bear on the allocation of national resources. It is not unreasonable to think that this may in part explain why middle-class diversions like tennis, golf, skiing and quadrophonic hi-fi have become national industries.

The practitioner as communicator

The public relations practitioner belongs to this group of middle-class communicators. If he is good at his job it is because he is an effective communicator; and if he is an effective communicator it is because he shares the values of those who control the media. This is not to say he is a slave of the media, but if he were at loggerheads with their view of social priorities he could not work with them. It is in this way that public relations contributes inevitably to social and cultural change. The public relations practitioner belongs to that group of people who dominate the new marketplace of ideas. Since the contribution made by the profession of public relations is the cumulative impact of that made by its individual practitioners, its quality and intensity depend on the practitioners. Quality and intensity in this context cannot be measured but they clearly depend on practitioners being aware of the social dimension of their work, and exercising discretion in the contribution they choose to make to it.

At the project level there are other qualitative objectives that cannot be overlooked. Creating awareness and changing attitudes are common objectives in public relations and neither can be measured convincingly with interval scales. Practitioners therefore often supplement surveys with other techniques, for example unstructured in-depth interviews with carefully selected people or before-and-after case studies of target communities based on personal observation. Clearly the findings of these tactics are no more precisely measurable than those of attitudinal surveys. The measurable element is the completion or non-completion of the interviews or case studies. Their results are therefore not suitable for computer analysis; but they are not meant for that. They are to be submitted to a team of human beings called Management who are able to process qualitative data.

4. Planning

Identification of Publics

A public is any distinguishable group of people (or individual person) with whom an organization has or should have a particular relationship. The organization does not have an identical relationship with each of its publics. A practitioner therefore does well to respect the principle that *in public relations each public is considered separately and as many individually styled relations as are necessary are established.* However, applying this principle can be an intimidating challenge.

Collectivities

To say that a public is a distinguishable group of people introduces two terms, 'public' and 'group', that need explaining; otherwise they may suggest nothing more specific than 'mob', 'crowd', 'team', 'gang', 'mass' or any equally vague term. Start with the general public. Although it is sometimes thought of as a homogenized population, it is actually made up of many smaller groups, each with distinguishing characteristics—income, education, age, sex, religion and so on. Individual people invariably belong to many such groups simultaneously. To some they belong by definition—age groups, for example; others they join voluntarily, such as political groups. The composition of a particular group, therefore, changes continually as people join or leave it. Furthermore, groups themselves sometimes coalesce into larger collectivities, or break down into smaller ones. In a crisis, for example, a number of small groups may join forces, whereas internal dissent may disintegrate a large group.

Sociologists generally describe collectivities as if they were arranged on a scale. At one end are those with a common purpose, internal coherence, strong organization and effective interaction among the members; the ideal might be called a 'team'. At the other end are groups of people who hardly know each other, seldom interact, and may not be aware of sharing a common purpose; in fact, they may not even realize they constitute a group. This type of collectivity is generally called a 'mass'. Between the team and the mass, human clusters are ranked according to their resemblance to one or the other extreme. The number of group-types identified on the scale depends on how subtly one wants to dissect the general public. Marketers sometimes carry segmentation to finely-tuned specificity.

Notice, from this point of view human clusters are not distinguished by size but by internal characteristics — particularly the sharing of a common purpose, and interaction among the group members. For logistic reasons size is also important in public relations planning, but the first concern has to be the nature of the group and the ways in which its members react to messages from outside. The principle stated above underlines the importance of directing public relations programmes to specific, coherent groups rather than to 'the mass'. The advantage of that approach can best be appreciated against a fuller description of just what a mass is.

Characteristics of the mass

(1) While a mass is usually widely dispersed, it has no set geographic boundaries. The territory it occupies may vary from one situation to another. The mass audience of one TV programme, for example, will differ from that of another.
(2) The composition of a mass can change. Immigration or employment opportunities, for example, can radically alter the composition of a town population.
(3) Because a mass has neither stable boundaries nor composition, the members have little incentive to get to know each other. They interact only haphazardly.
(4) Since the members don't know each other and interact casually, they generally have no sense of common identity.
(5) The members of a mass are held together more by external circumstances than by personal characteristics — by their common interest in football, for example, rather than similar personality traits.
(6) Because their individual differences have been at least temporarily repressed, the members of a mass react to stimulation in patterned ways. Their behaviour is seldom uniform, but its variations are quite predictable — because they lack subtlety; mass reactions fall into a few unrefined, clearly distinct categories — agree-disagree, like-dislike and so on.

This description might suggest that mass members are near-zombies. Fortunately this is not so. But their resistance to homogenizing influences comes less from personal qualities than from small-group loyalties. In response to an unrefined public relations programme, a Socialist's individual personality probably won't assert itself, but his political party loyalties may do so. Similarly, allegiance to neighbourhood, religion or professional affiliation can resist a drift towards unthinking mass reactions. If, therefore, a public relations programme is not atuned to specific group interests, people will likely respond to it as members of a mass, that is, without any personal interest. This seldom works to the public relations practitioner's advantage.

The alternative

In place of the word 'group' let us now substitute the term 'public'—to respect the jargon of public relations. Ideally, in public relations planning one would like to appeal to the individual interests of each member of a public being addressed. But this is not feasible. The challenge, therefore, is to address publics large enough to achieve cost-efficiency, yet sufficiently specialized to ensure effective communication. No public relations programme will appeal to all publics; but a programme can be designed to appeal strongly to a particular one. The limited size of a particular public and its special interests make it possible for the practitioner to study the attitudes and behaviour of its members. He can read the magazines they read, visit the places they frequent, talk with them, get to know their likes and dislikes, their interests, ambitions, fears and other dispositions. He can also discover the channels of communication that link them to other publics. On that basis, he stands a good chance of designing an effective programme.

Criteria for distinguishing publics

To say that a public is 'distinguishable' means that its members are marked by certain characteristics that identify them and set them apart from other people. But these characteristics are not always readily discernible. It is generally easy to distinguish men from women, but many publics are distinguished by traits that are difficult to detect and impossible to measure. What, for example, is a 'hippie'? He is an unorthodox individual; he belongs to a social group who share unconventional values; and through his group membership he helps perpetuate a culture of spiritual marginality. He is very different from a fascist by any name. But defining a hippie in a way that clearly distinguishes him from all other people is not easy. Sodomites are as unorthodox as hippies; vegetarians' values are as unconventional as hippies'; mystics, like hippies, perpetuate a culture of spiritual marginality. The world is peopled with a bewildering variety of social and cultural types who share certain characteristics, are poles apart on others and evolve constantly. Anyone interested in sorting them out (and that, up to a point, is what a public relations practitioner must do) therefore needs an organizing principle. He needs a perspective comprehensive enough to encompass the diversity of the human species but simple enough to be helpful. He needs a point of view that will allow him to arrange his observations in a meaningful order, to recognize similarities, trends and significant departures. A simple curiosity in respect to human diversity is not enough. The public relations practitioner is guided by the demands of his job; in other words, his professional purpose sets his perspective. He seeks to identify publics either: (a) because his organization already has a natural or committed relationship with them; or (b) because the organization should have a special relationship with them; or (c) because the organization is searching for new publics with which it might possibly establish special relationships. The objectives of a particular project may temporarily sharpen the focus of his concern (for example, he may be interested only in middle-aged churchgoers), but for the moment consider his continuing task of identifying all those publics of actual or possible interest to his organization.

The first step
Although guided by his professional purpose and equipped with a thorough understanding of the organization, he still needs a directive to help him take the first step. Many practitioners find it in responding to questions like: Who would be affected if my organization went out of business? Whose livelihood depends in any way on the organization? Who addresses any form of communication to the organization? To whom could the organization conceivably become useful? For each organization mentioned in my appointments diary, how many similar organizations exist?

Alternatively, the practitioner might start by studying the structure and functions of his own organization. Each department within the organization has its own specific functions and each of these functions generates a cluster of publics. But could these publics, now functionally related to the organization, be related to it in any other way?

Studying publics
Assuming that a certain line of inquiry leads the practitioner to identify a number of publics, he then wants to study each of

them. An organization cannot effectively communicate with a public it does not understand. The practitioner therefore gets to know the public's constituent elements and how they relate to each other. He wants to know what holds them together. Generally the members of a public are united in sharing common values or purposes. What are these values and purposes in the public under study? How does it pursue its purposes, in other words, how does it operate? All these questions relate to the structure and functions of the public, but of equal importance are the attitudes of its members. Are they conservative or innovative? favourably disposed to his own organization or opposed to it? Are they intellectual; politically motivated; creative; ambitious; religiously inclined; resistant to change; narrow-minded; lethargic; and so on. Then too, there are a number of basic descriptive variables by which publics are often distinguished—age, sex, education, income level, scope of responsibility, etc.

Many publics, once identified and described, can then be subdivided. An organization's employees, for example, might include management, administrative staff, clerical workers, manual labourers, full-time and part-time employees, permanent employees and casual workers, shareholders and non-shareholders; and all of these subdivisions might be further segmented by department—sales, marketing, personnel etc. Each subdivision might at times be treated as a separate public, at other times it may be included in some configuration of publics.

It is impossible to list all the criteria by which publics might possibly be distinguished; nor is it necessary. As stated earlier, each practitioner is ultimately guided by his own purposes. The point in listing criteria at all is simply to suggest the practicability of the principle that individual publics be identified for particular treatment.

Monitoring publics
In effective public relations individual publics are not only identified and studied, they are continually monitored thereafter. Publics evolve: they are composed of living people whose attitudes are constantly modified by experience and natural development. New publics emerge and combine with existing ones the way atoms combine to form molecules. Sometimes in the process certain publics undergo fundamental change or simply go out of existence. The most rigorous study of a public's attitudes is never anything more than a time-bound perception, a moment in an ever-changing life. Generally too, an organization evolves: steady-state systems are rare. And the relationship between two evolving systems—an organization and any one of its publics—is

necessarily dynamic. In public relations, things are never fully under control.

Reaching particular publics

All we have said so far relates to an organization's continuing need to identify and understand its publics. But in planning a particular project the identification of publics is more sharply focused. Few public relations projects are directed to all an organization's publics at once. Much more commonly they are designed to reach individual publics or limited clusters of them. It is a strategy motivated by more than efficiency. No doubt resources can be wasted in projects that are unthinkingly diffuse rather than carefully aimed. But the end result of a blunderbuss approach could be that no-one is affected by the project. We will see later in this chapter that the response to a communication depends very much on the character and dispositions of the receiver. The same applies to a public. If the message is not adapted to its special character and mentality it might have no effect whatsoever. A project intended to affect everyone might very well affect no one. To the degree that it is necessary or helpful, therefore, the practitioner adapts his project design to the requirements of the specific public or publics it is intended to reach.

The danger now is to go too far in the opposite direction — from the ineffective blunderbuss approach to one equally ineffective because it fails to take into account the social environment of the public in question. A public does not exist in isolation. Almost invariably it interacts with other publics. Frequently the interaction is essential to its own existence. If there were no publics called 'patients' there could be none called 'doctors'. To some degree, doctors are defined by patients. Therefore, a project directed to doctors (as doctors) has to accommodate their special relationship to patients, otherwise it is unrealistic. However, given the complexity of social life, is it possible to define the social context of a public without getting drawn into a maze? Where do you stop in constructing a social context? On this point, public relations practitioners might take a lesson from social workers and what they call the Integrated Model.

The Integrated Model

The social worker can be defined as a public relations practitioner in some ways. On four counts the work parallels that of a professional consultant:

(1) Social workers are concerned with the quality of human

relationships, and assign high priority to the development of mutual understanding between clients and their publics;

(2) The social worker's contact with clients is usually direct, person-to-person;

(3) In most cases social workers intervene in a situation in order to solve a problem or take advantage of an opportunity, and they are constantly guided by that orientation in developing and implementing strategies;

(4) The social worker's standard practice is to identify the individual publics of concern in a situation—those who by their composition and function affect the definition of the situation or the best approach to it.

It may seem, therefore, that the social worker could learn a lot from public relations practitioners; which may be true. However, given the urgency and sometimes traumatic nature of the problems faced by social workers, they seem to search more assiduously than public relations practitioners for innovative approaches to their work. By their own admission they have no pat answers or magic formulae, and every one of the various models proposed to guide their practice has its shortcomings. Still, the literature on social work methods has much to offer the public relations practitioner—for example, the model we are now considering.

Much was written about the Integrated Model in the 1970s and among its better-known exponents at that time were A Pincus and A Minahan (1973) whose work is still highly respected. These two authors visualised the individual person as continually drawing material and emotional resources from a variety of social systems. The social worker, therefore, intervening to help solve an individual's problem must consider the systems on which the client depends. Pincus and Minahan identified four principal systems in any problematic situation: the Client System, the Target System, the Action System and the Change Agent System. (The four function in the larger Social System.) Before discussing each of them, let us substitute the term 'public' for 'system'. Unfortunately 'public' is a less dynamic term but we are used to it and it will help clarify the application of the model to public relations.

Application to public relations
The Client Public is the individual, group or community suffering from the problem of concern. Consider an example: student dissatisfaction in a college was traced to the inability of teachers to instruct them in new technologies. It was clear that the teachers in question needed updated training. Therefore, a principal objective of the proposed solution was that the teachers should attend short, intensive courses to update their skills. The

53

dissatisfied students constituted the Client Public in this case. It was their problem that Management wanted to eliminate. Interestingly, a social worker (student welfare officer) would have discussed the problem with the students first—the client's views and expectations are considered that important. But the student dissatisfaction came from the inadequacy of one of their resource systems—the teachers who were unable to offer them the courses they wanted. The teachers, then, were part of the Target Public, that is, those people who would have to be involved if the objectives of the problem-solving project were to be achieved. In some situations there may be several groups and key individuals included in the Target Public. In addition to its tactical advantages, the distinction between the Client Public and the Target Public has an important spin-off benefit: it reassures the client that it is not being taken for granted that the problem lies entirely with him.

Thirdly there is the Action Public which comprises 'those with whom the social worker deals...to accomplish the tasks and achieve the goals of the change effort' (Pincus & Minahan, 1973, p.61). These are the people who have the authority, responsibility and resources to take action. In the case we are considering, the public relations practitioner would at very least have had to deal with the government department where decisions would be made and budgets allocated, the universities which would be asked to provide courses for the teachers, and the department responsible for producing, for example, instructional video films for the teachers. Possibly other groups would also have been included in the Action Public; in particular, 'power structures' spring to mind—those groups of people who, officially or unofficially, are able to 'get things done'.

Finally there is the Change Agent Public which in our example would have comprised the public relations practitioner himself and his agency, as well as any others who might have served as advisors.

The practitioner as catalyst

Following this model, a public relations practitioner would function as a catalyst, directing the resources of a Change Agent Public, an Action Public and a Target Public to solving the problem of a Client Public (in the example, the college students). He himself would be but a single element in an interactive network of problem-solving publics. He would function at the point where the four publics overlap, deriving from each of them an enrichment of his own limited problem-solving capacities. Pincus and Minahan see this as contributing to a broader definition of the social worker's purpose. In the Integrated Model the social worker would operate to:

(1) Enhance the problem-solving capacities of people;
(2) Link people with the systems that provide them with resources, services and opportunities;
(3) Promote the effective and humane operation of these systems;
(4) Contribute to the development and improvement of social policy (Pincus & Minahan, 1973, p.9).

The first three of these could be directly applied to the function of the public relations practitioner; clearly they all depend on a mutual understanding between the involved publics. The fourth purpose would have to be modified according to the situation. The practitioner is naturally concerned with policy implications, but they could be any policies—governmental or those of the participating publics, including his own agency.

The model would not apply in every public relations situation but it would be worth the effort to identify those where it could work. And whenever applied, it would be wise to explain it to the client. The client's confidence in the practitioner is crucial to the success of any public relations project and this would be better assured if it were made clear that the practitioner is approaching the problem with an open mind. He is neither the blind functionary of an oracular agency nor an omniscient wizard who has no need to consult others. He operates in a liaison capacity between all the participating publics, including his own agency (the Change Agent Public). According to this model, the students in our example would have discussed with the practitioner the goals and targets to be set for the intervention, and only after that would they *together* have identified the Action Public. This would almost certainly have won the students' confidence. It might also have helped them to appreciate the limits of what could be done to solve their problem.

Structured spontaneity
But the final ingenuity of the Integrated Model is in its paradoxical structuring of spontaneity. Its structured aspect lends itself to organized planning, while its respect for the contribution of each participating public opens the way to unforeseen possibilities. In its application to public relations it would set the practitioner's contribution to problem solving into a highly creative context. He might learn more than he would contribute, but it would be his catalysing function that would make the learning possible.

The Integrated Model is not proposed here as the final solution to the public relations problem of dealing with publics in their social context. But it does illustrate one way of creatively organizing clusters of publics to solve a problem.

Intermediate Objectives

In the process of designing a project, intermediate objectives generally suggest themselves to planners as logical stepping stones to final objectives. But it does not always happen like that. The process is not necessarily linear. Sometimes it begins with an intermediate objective, the final objective then being seen as a desirable consequent possibility. Or an organization might first identify a public it wants to attract, planners then being asked to develop a project to achieve that end. No matter how the process evolves, however, it is important to respect the relationship of intermediate objectives to final objectives. In the example cited above (college students dissatisfied because their teachers could not instruct them in new technologies), two main objectives were set for the problem-solving project:

(1) To establish a teacher-training programme in new technologies;
(2) To eliminate student dissatisfaction.

Clearly the attainment of the second objective depended on the attainment of the first. The second was therefore the final objective, the first the intermediate objective. The relationship of a final objective to an intermediate objective is one of dependence. Long-term and short-term objectives, on the other hand, are related temporally. Short-term objectives are expected to be attained before long-term ones, but the latter do not necessarily depend on the former.

Justifying intermediate objectives

While intermediate objectives may seem reasonable to planners, they may not immediately appear so to those who pass judgement on the project proposal. In the give-and-take of planning sessions logical justifications are made explicit and their strength is tested in debate. But if these justifications are not spelled out in the project document, appraisers might question the proposal's logical coherence. In the dissatisfied-students case, there was no inherent connection between the teacher-training programme and student dissatisfaction — some metaphysical link that no sensible person could question. The connection was purely logical; its reasonableness was derived from the causes of the student dissatisfaction. The project proposal therefore had to make it clear that the teacher-training programme would elim- inate those causes. If that requirement seems petty, remember that although the student dissatisfaction originated in their teachers' ignorance of new technologies, it might later have developed additional roots. Conceivably the students' negative attitude opened their eyes to other things they disliked about their teachers. If that was so, then the problem would not be elim- inated simply by improving the teachers' qualifications. And if the dissatisfaction persisted after the upgrading courses had been completed, the teachers (now with improved qualifications) might leave the school and find better employment elsewhere. The final situation would be worse than the original one.

It therefore had to be convincingly demonstrated in the project proposal that the causes of student dissatisfaction would be entirely eliminated through the teacher-training programme. If that had not been possible, then perhaps additional intermediate objectives would have had to be built into the project. Many a proposal has been rejected by potential funders on the grounds that the logical justifications for intermediate objectives were not evident. A firm principle should, therefore, be that *in public relations project proposals the logical connections between inter- mediate and final objectives are explicitly stated.* Unfortunately this frequently does not happen.

Logic

Justifications may be weighted with emotion but if they cannot stand up to cold brutal analysis they will be rejected. The empha- sis must be on logic. Logic is a style of reasoning guided by the principles and structures of sound thought. It is therefore viewed as valid. Logic is a recognized branch of philosophy with formally drawn rules and structures. But it is not necessary to bring in a logician to check the coherence of a proposal, it is enough that it be carefully drawn up by clear-thinking people. Unfortunately not everyone who occupies a position of authority is clear-thinking.

Deductive reasoning

Logicians distinguish two types of reasoning—deductive and inductive. In deduction one argues from a general observation to a particular instance of it. Consider an example: shortly before an election, a prominent member of one of the contending parties is convicted of illegal and scandalous behaviour—clearly a setback for the party. The election campaign manager suggests that in

57

their speeches candidates make no direct reference to the scandal but concentrate more than ever on the fundamental principles of democracy, the party's basic ideology in that context, and its history of commendable public service. He is opposed by some members who advise that the party leader should face the scandal squarely, bring it out in the open, dissociate the party from what happened and win points for honesty and courage. Two irreconcilable proposals, each in some way commendable, both risky. A choice must be made soon otherwise the inconsistent behaviour of campaigning candidates could make matters worse.

Suppose the campaign manager then defended his proposal in this way: 'It is an established fact that fundamental beliefs, like political and religious ones, are more stable than attitudes derived from recent experience. Therefore, if in this case we appeal to people's belief in democracy and the principles of our party, our campaign will have a strong enough base to resist the less stable negative attitudes triggered by this scandal.' Unless those who opposed this point of view could support their case with similarly logical argument, the campaign manager's proposal would stand the better chance of being accepted.

Notice that he brings no new information to the argument. He states a widely accepted principle—that fundamental beliefs are more stable than attitudes triggered by experience—and shows that his proposal is an application of it. In other words, the conclusion of his argument was already contained in its main premise; he simply made it explicit. This type of argument is powerful because it presents people with a conclusion they already implicitly accept if they accept the general premise on which the argument is based. This is not to say that the conclusion of a deductive argument is always true. Logic and truth are two different things. If the premises of a logical argument are true the conclusion will be true; if any of the premises are false the conclusion will be false, even if the logic is solid. If you believe that all Japanese products are free from manufacturing defects and you believe this camera to be Japanese, you will logically think it is well made. But you may be mistaken in thinking either that all Japanese products are reliable or that this camera is Japanese. Your reasoning is logical but the premises are not necessarily true. A sound argument is both logical and true.

In Chapter 1 it was said that public relations deals more often with probabilities than with certainties. Does this mean that a practitioner, even though using impeccable logic, can rarely be sure of the soundness of his proposals because he can seldom guarantee the truth of his arguments? A proposal always includes a number of verifiable facts which must be true, a number of probabilities which must be strong, and a few general principles dependable enough to be considered true. A proposal, even though perfectly logical, can never be stronger than the probabilities on which it is based. At what point does a probability become strong enough to serve as a premise of a proposal? The practitioner must make that judgement himself.

In a public relations proposal we are not merely trying to demonstrate the reasonableness of a conclusion, we are usually trying to get approval for a course of action. Deductive reasoning offers special advantages in that case. First of all, by relating a specific problem to an already accepted general principle, the problem becomes more understandable; it is no longer just an isolated bit of information, but can now be seen in a context that gives it meaning. The campaign manager referred to above made the political scandal more comprehensible as an element in the campaign. He showed that it was not an explosion that had immeasurably damaged the party's election chances; rather, it was an incident whose limited effects could be estimated and assessed in the light of certain principles derived from broad-based experience.

In addition, deductive reasoning makes a proposed action more acceptable by relating it to an accepted general principle. The general principle provides a more secure ground for action than does a particular situation: it bases the proposed action on universal experience. Deductive reasoning points out to the client that his acceptance of a proposed action would be an endorsement of a solid principle.

Inductive reasoning

The most common alternative to deductive reasoning is induction. Induction reverses the direction of deduction; it argues from particular cases to a general principle. Induction says: 'This case we are considering is like one we had last year, it's the same problem that five of our competitors have had over the past few years. And in each previous case the solution we are now proposing worked. It therefore seems reasonable to assume that it generally works.' Notice that the conclusion is not certain (as the conclusion of a deductive argument is), it is only probable. But the more cases you can put forward to support it the stronger its probability becomes. Nevertheless, it takes only one defeat to destroy the argument. If, in the example, the proposed solution once failed to eliminate the problem, it would be illogical to assume that it always works; clearly it does not always work. And even if it has never yet failed, you cannot be sure that it never will. The conclusion of an inductive argument is always only a probability.

Induction is seldom used alone. It is usually combined with deduction. In the example above, if the client accepted the principle that the proposed solution generally works, then you would argue deductively from that generality to your specific case: 'Since the solution generally works, it should work in our case.'

Induction may appear to be a weaker style of reasoning than deduction because the conclusion is never certain. But few things in life are certain and it is not unreasonable to act on strong probability. You can make a very good case for a proposed problem solution by citing a number of instances in which it has worked well.

Induction is particularly helpful in policy formation. Policy is the link between general principle and operational procedure. It guides practice but must be supported by principle; and general principle is supported by the number of particular cases in which its reliability has been demonstrated. Here, for example, is a well-known general principle: 'A satisfied customer is a good advertisement.' The corresponding policy is: 'We must do everything possible to satisfy our customers.' The application of this policy then shows up in the way the company conducts its business. The general principle is the point of departure and by inductive reasoning it becomes stronger as the number of cases supporting it increases. It also becomes more powerful if the supporting cases are not all identical. Policy proposal, or a proposed refinement of existing policy, can therefore be very well supported by inductive reasoning.

Obviously a proposal should in its entirety be a logical statement, but the clarity of reasoning must be especially evident in linking proposed intermediate to final objectives and all objectives to identified problems. Those are the links that ultimately carry the decision on the acceptability of a plan.

Communication, the Constant Objective

Communication is the transfer of messages. Whatever one says about it beyond that is elaboration. Communication studies often concentrate on:

(1) the cognitive or emotional content of the messages;
(2) the ways in which they are encoded for transmission — visible signs, sounds, electrical impulses etc;
(3) the technologies used to transfer them from point to point;
(4) the social structures (political, economic etc) that control the media and access to them;
(5) the reactions of people receiving the messages, and their psychological, social and cultural determinants.

The job of a public relations practitioner is to see to it that the organization he works for gets along well with its publics. In other words he seeks to establish and maintain healthy relationships. In doing so, he inevitably functions as both a sender and receiver of messages, because a relationship is a communication complex. It is not something merely supported by communication. It is itself a continuous exchange of messages, a continuing, multi-faceted communication between its constituent elements. Human relationships are extremely subtle. They sometimes survive, even intensify, without any exchange of perceptible messages between the parties involved—silence being the message. Conceivably that could happen in the relationships between an organization and its publics because they are essentially human relationships, but it is more prudent to assume that they depend very much on the controlled exchange of carefully prepared messages. On that basis, communications planning invariably features prominently in the planning of any public relations project.

Persuasive communication
The public relations practitioner makes it his job to understand all aspects of the communication process and the ways in which it is affected by social and cultural circumstances. He does this, however, not as an uninvolved scholar. As in all other aspects of his job he is guided by his professional purpose—to persuade groups of people (publics) to participate in the creation and maintenance of congenial relationships with his client. He therefore has a special interest in a particular type of communication called 'persuasive communication'. It includes all the elements of any other communication type but the heart of the message is a proposal submitted for acceptance by the receiver. The proposal may be explicit or implied, it might relate to behaviour, attitude, belief or understanding. But its acceptance or rejection is always the result of a process that is anything but simple.

Many practitioners underestimate the complexity of the persuasive communication process. In planning a project they assume that if publics have been carefully identified and have the facts straight they will think, feel and behave in ways that will benefit their relationship with the organization; it is just a matter of giving them the right information. Unfortunately communication research over the past 20 years has confirmed that the linkages between knowledge, attitudes and behaviour are not that straightforward. The three sometimes pull against each other, which is why people at times have to admit, 'I knew I shouldn't have done that,' or 'I hate to do this but...' And even when the three seem to be in harmony, generally each has its own determinants. A change in one does not necessarily bring about a change in the others. All of which means that a public relations programme based on an assumed alliance between knowledge, attitudes and behaviour might well prove ineffective, or could even make things worse.

Persuasive communication model
In 1953 Carl Hovland and his research team at Yale University proposed a model comprising six basic steps in the process of persuasion: exposition, attention, comprehension, acceptance/ rejection, persistence and finally action. But even that model was found lacking. It could not reliably predict the effects of messages received, nor could it adequately explain the success or failure of persuasive communications. Later researchers refined the model and in the late 1960s an interesting new element was introduced — one that remains today as a powerful (although hypothetical) key factor in the process of persuasion. It is a set of internal reactions to messages received, reactions termed 'cognitive responses'. It is a term worth remembering as it often appears in the literature; and it is a concept worth understanding because it so logically explains and confidently predicts the effects of persuasive communications. Let us start at the beginning of the process with the problem of getting the attention of people we want to persuade.

Getting attention

When you enter a newsagent's shop and find yourself almost surrounded by racks of magazines, you ignore most of them no matter how attractive their covers. And when you choose one and flip through it, you scarcely notice most of the advertisements; you give your attention only to those that interest you. Of all the direct-mail pieces you receive at home, how many do you read carefully? How many do you read at all? Messages are most often received the way a newsvendor at a busy junction receives traffic sounds; he doesn't even sort them out, they are simply part of the background. Giving attention to a message is the exception, not the rule.

The public relations practitioner might rebut: 'But a communicator can't do more than his best. If he's done that, he has to leave the rest in the hands of the gods.' But what is one's best? If you realize what happens the moment your intended receiver is tapped by your message, there are things you can do in advance to increase the likelihood that he will pay attention to it.

Criteria for selection
To say that people give their attention to some messages but

not to others raises the question: on what basis do they select? Researchers studying this question were first guided by some common occurrences. For example, anti-tobacco ads are more often read by non-smokers than by smokers. Most of those who attend Conservative party rallies are Conservatives. Environmental protection demonstrations are attended by people already concerned about the environment. In other words, people apparently choose to give their attention to messages with which they already agree.

This observation led to the hypothesis that our selection is defensive. It was suggested that we search out information that confirms our views and avoid that which opposes them. However, in the late 1960s a battery of experiments designed to test this proposition failed to come up with the resounding support expected. The findings indicated that we do not choose messages with which we agree simply because they support our present opinions. Our selection is based on other criteria. It is just a coincidence that in being guided by those other criteria we acquire information that most often *also* confirms our present views. Furthermore, there was little evidence in the research findings to suggest that we avoid information that challenges our present opinions. Researchers were, in fact, struck by the frequency with which participants in experiments gave their attention to messages opposing their viewpoints in preference to those which were supportive. It seemed unlikely they would do this simply because they could not resist the challenge of a confrontation. There must, the researchers thought, be more pedestrian reasons. From a series of subsequent experiments, four hypotheses survived with considerable strength.

First, people prefer useful to useless information. This is most evident in situations where the receiver of a message is involved in the process. For example, the information might be useful for a specific task (how to cultivate a vegetable garden) or for the assumption of a role (a new mother caring for her baby).

Secondly, people look for information that reduces or eliminates uncertainty — for which most of us have a rather low tolerance. A person emotionally very much opposed to the development of nuclear energy might nevertheless be uncertain of the factual basis for his opposition; he would be likely to look for information to eliminate his uncertainty. (Since this information would also be useful to him, this second proposition overlaps the previous one.)

Thirdly, we often seek out information which we know is preferred by those whose opinions we respect. If someone we admire subscribes to a particular magazine, we might also subscribe. If our idol is a health food enthusiast we might look for information on that subject. (This touches on the question of opinion leadership treated in Chapter 2.)

Finally, we are attracted more to messages that arouse our curiosity than to those which are timeworn and familiar.

Preaching to the converted
Guided by these criteria, people generally select messages without giving thought to whether they support or oppose their views. Which is all very interesting but does not explain why, as a rule, persuasive messages are most often read by those who don't need to be persuaded, people who already accept the proposed point of view. The explanation lies partly in the fact that useful information or that which reduces uncertainty might also support our existing opinions; and information preferred by those we respect as opinion leaders would probably conform to our own views. But these observations fall short of a complete explanation. A somewhat stronger one lies in the availability of information. People most often choose supportive information simply because it is more available to them than challenging material. Whenever possible we prefer to spend our time with people whose opinions we share. People with strong left-wing views generally associate with others of the same disposition, they browse leftist bookstores, belong to leftist associations. They live in a world of their own choosing, not beyond the reach of opposition but certainly in friendly territory. They exchange information on what is happening in that world, inform each other of coming events of interest. They subscribe to leftist magazines and, once on the mailing list, receive information about causes, events, books etc of interest to like-minded people. Not surprisingly then, they receive more leftist information than rightist.

We are still short of a full explanation for the bothersome fact that public relations practitioners often find themselves either preaching to the converted or being ignored by the uninterested. But research findings do at least suggest tactics by which communications might be modified to attract greater interest. It would be helpful, for example, if the message reflected the values of the leaders of the public of interest, or offered useful information in a way that assured certainty. The practitioner should bear in mind too that just as people associate with like-minded people, publics associate with like-minded publics. For example, people in radio associate more often with those in television than they do with university professors, and ecumenical sentiments often bring together the clergy of various religious denominations.

Experimentation

But for all that, it is myopic and dangerous to distil magic formulae from the 'discoveries' of communication research. Granted, the temptation is strong because our own yen for certainty is as pressing as that of our publics. But we have to accept the limitations of science. Most of what is known about people's reactions to messages is based on experiments. A sample of people is drawn from a certain population (often university students) to be tested under highly abnormal conditions. For example, to test the influence of distraction on giving attention to a message, the subjects might be isolated in a sound-proof semi-darkened room where the only disturbances are a taped voice delivering the message and a small irregularly blinking light meant to distract. The idea is to control all other circumstances in order to measure the single influence of distraction. But the result is a situation so bizarre that one hesitates to apply the findings of the experiment to the enormous variety of people receiving publicity messages daily at Piccadilly Circus or Times Square.

The public relations practitioner therefore preserves a guarded respect for the findings of scientific research, especially those of the social sciences which necessarily deal with probabilities rather than certainties. Yet every public relations project is in some way an application of such findings. It is therefore a principle that *public relations projects are always pretested before full implementation*. The pretest seldom verifies the perfect applicability of research findings in the project but it indicates the likelihood of their applicability. Often too, it suggests ways in which they could be refined before being applied.

Acceptance or rejection

Assuming you have succeeded in gaining the attention of the person for whom your message is intended, what happens next? A person does not receive a persuasive communication as he might accept directions on how to get to a bus stop. Persuasive messages are received as propositions asking for acceptance, and they activate a psychological process in the recipient. A normal person's immediate response is judgemental. After all, it rarely happens that we propose concepts about which people know absolutely nothing, or on which they have no existing attitudes whatsoever. When they are received, persuasive messages (for example, those of public relations) usually find themselves immediately confronted by an assembly of beliefs, attitudes, evaluations, expectations and cognitions all well established in the mind of the receiver and all related to the subject at hand. Responses to the uninvited presence, the message, are the 'cognitive responses' referred to earlier. (The word 'cognitive' is actually too restrictive in this context but it is entrenched in the jargon.)

Cognitive responses
It is not that our stock of beliefs, attitudes, expectations etc vote on the acceptance or rejection of a proposition, the majority vote carrying the day; the process is described rather as a series of sequential decisions. The first decision might relate, for example, to the credibility of the source of the message. If the source is accepted as credible, the proposition advances to the second position—perhaps the tone of the message: is it irritating, disarming, intriguing? If again accepted, the proposition advances further. When, in this series of appraisals, the rational content of the message is examined the cognitive responses submit counter-arguments drawn from the recipient's reservoir of self-defences. These counter-arguments may be reasoned, but need not be; they could be purely emotional, based on unreasoned belief, or subtle countering combinations, which means that the simple understanding of a message, even a perfectly logical one, is not enough to assure its acceptance; nor is memorization of the message (contrary to common belief). A communication may be well enough understood to trigger a powerful counter-argument that will cause the message to be remembered but rejected nonetheless. As a rule, only new information on which the receiver has no established attitudes and therefore no cognitive responses is accepted hospitably, for example most information given to students in their courses.

The hope of the communicator is, of course, that his proposition will survive the complete series of challenges and finally be accepted. However, since the cognitive priorities of various publics—indeed, of individual people—can differ, the strategies for survival must be carefully planned. As soon as the proposal encounters a negative response it faces the possibility of rejection, in which case the persuasive communication will have failed. Only the support of a disposition more powerful and stable than the one in opposition can prevent this.

Preserving the status quo
Admittedly there is an air of conservatism to this theory. According to it we are not persuaded by the messages we receive, we are persuaded by our own responses which are simply activated by incoming messages. And since these responses are self-defensive the theory seems to predict the preservation of the status quo, which is apparently bad news for the public relations practitioner

faced with the task of motivating change. But the cause is not lost, by any means.

We don't, after all, want to drain the entire reservoir of a person's existing dispositions and replenish it with a freshly brewed mix of our own. In fact we count very much on the relative stability of people's attitudes and forms of behaviour. They are the basis of loyalty. When we propose, therefore, the acceptance of a new disposition or form of behaviour, we must set the proposition in a context of favourable dispositions already firmly established in the minds of those we are addressing. We must appeal to existing attitudes, beliefs and opinions on whose support we can depend. Here we encounter the question of levels of stability.

Levels of stability

A person apparently indifferent to the physical torture inflicted on political prisoners in some countries, might nevertheless be persuaded to support Amnesty International if the appeal was on the basis of a universal inalienable right to freedom of opinion. The value assigned to the concept of freedom in such a case would have shown itself to be strong enough and stable enough to carry the proposal all the way to acceptance in spite of relatively weak cognitive responses opposing it. The telling power of an effective communicator, therefore, is not in his access to the media or in his mastery of communication techniques; it is in his capacity to set the terms in which propositions are to be discussed. If those terms constitute a favourable environment for his proposal it will likely be accepted.

The public relations practitioner who presents the 'right' information to the public, hoping his point of view will be accepted, is not being unreasonable. It is obviously necessary that the information be 'right'. But that is not enough. Several other things must also be 'right', for example the source of the information, its emotional flavour, its relevance, the way it touches the respondent's experience or belief system. For each of these factors there is a cognitive response waiting to pass judgement on the proposal. The carrying power of each response depends on its level of stability. There are people who would reject an impeccably logical proposition simply because the style of expression smacked of inappropriate humour. The effective public relations communicator therefore discovers the points of anchorage in the dispositions of his public, whether that public be a national population or one single, very important person. And his message is finely modulated to win acceptance on those key points. His principle is that *a proposition will be accepted only if it is compatible with the strongest dispositions of the public to which it is submitted.*

But even if it is accepted, will the public act on it? Perhaps not; there are pitfalls between the acceptance of a 'good idea' and its translation into action.

Knowledge and feelings

At the end of a political campaign by Candidate X, the vote you cast for or against him is the final expression of a negotiated agreement between what you know about him and how you feel about him. (Admittedly, party loyalty might also influence your vote, but that need not concern us here.) Think of these as two dimensions of your attitude towards him—the intellectual dimension (what you know) and the emotional dimension (how you feel). That these are two distinct responses can hardly be questioned; our daily experience confirms it. You may agree with the views of Candidate X but find that your intellectual acceptance of his message is vetoed by your feelings against him: 'I don't know what it is, but something about his manner puts me off. I don't trust him.' Similarly you may agree that women should have the right to abortion on demand but your feelings might persuade you to vote against the legalization of that view.

Cognitive dissonance
Usually the two dimensions are in harmony. When one changes the other generally changes in the same direction, but not always. Each has its own determinants. That is why many people, although convinced of the link between cigarettes and cancer, continue to smoke because they like it. But why are convictions and feelings usually in harmony? Because we are not happy when we suffer from psychological discord. A conflict between what we know and how we feel can be so tormenting that, if necessary, we will force a reconciliation between the two. For example, your emotional distrust of Candidate X might motivate you to scrutinize the details of his political stance in order to find grounds for rejecting it. Or, conversely, you might try to warm up to him emotionally by searching for likeable traits.

In some cases one is forced to act on the basis of either feelings or reason before a reconciliation between the two has been negotiated. The psychological state which results from this was called 'cognitive dissonance' by Leon Festinger in *A Theory of Cognitive Dissonance* (1957, Row Peterson, Evanston Ill). It can be unpleasant enough to intensify the effort to find a harmonious internal coherence. A vegetarian might, for example, eat a steak rather than offend a host who has honoured him with a dinner. The guest will then find some intellectually satisfying grounds for having ranked his feelings for his host above his feelings against eating meat. It is not important, by the way, that the internal coherence be logical, only that it be satisfying.

Changing emotions
The public relations practitioner is concerned with maintaining harmonious relationships between his organization and its publics. What can he do if a public harbours negative feelings towards the organization in spite of a general acceptance of its policies and operation? Is there some way he can change the emotional dimension of the public attitude without disturbing the positive intellectual dimension? In other words, how can one favourably change public feelings?

There are only two possibilities: either you reach people's feelings by giving them emotionally charged facts, or you bypass their intelligence and touch their feelings directly. The first is the more common approach. If people dislike an organization although accepting what they know about it, it could be that they don't know enough or that they don't know the right things. As a rule, people's feelings about someone depend largely on the attributes which they know that person possesses. Their feelings for the attribute 'honesty', for example, rub off onto the honest person. The person is then liked—first because the attribute is liked, and secondly because it is believed that the person possesses the attribute. In 1975 these two factors led a researcher named Fishbein to devise a mathematical formula for assessing a person's feelings towards something (see Fishbein, M and Ajzen, I *Belief, Attitude, Intention and Behaviour*, 1975, Addison-Wesley Publishing Co, Reading, Mass.):

$$E = DA \times V$$

E stands for evaluation (ie, one's feelings for or against), DA stands for the degree to which you believe the person or thing possesses a given attribute, and V stands for the value you assign to that attribute. For example, if an advertisement states that a certain skin cream will eliminate wrinkles, your feelings for or against that cream will depend on (1) how important the elimination of wrinkles is for you and (2) how strongly you believe that the cream actually will eliminate them. Multiply the two factors together and you've got a measure of your feelings about the cream. If there are many attributes to be considered, Fishbein says you should calculate this combination for each one then add them all together:

$$E = DA_1 \times V_1 + DA_2 \times V_2 + DA_n \times V_n$$

It is a formula that takes some time to apply. It is therefore hard to believe that people actually put themselves through this mental exercise before deciding whether to buy a product. Later researchers suggested that perhaps people evaluate products on the basis of a single key attribute rather than on all of them; or they choose a product that surpasses others on at least one attribute. Unfortunately none of these approaches is fully satisfying, but they all helpfully stress the connection between a product's known attributes and people's feelings towards it. Applying this principle to public relations is straightforward. One must ensure that all the organization's attributes are publicly known. If collectively they generate negative feelings then the organization has serious internal problems that go beyond the scope of public relations.

The direct approach

Consider now the second approach. If what is publicly known about an organization leaves people indifferent or negatively disposed, is there some way to reach their feelings directly? Let's start by saying that there is no convincing experimental support for this approach. That does not rule it out as an alternative but it makes it risky. There are three tactics that sometimes work:

Association

Examples from advertising are perhaps most illustrative. If rum can be associated strongly enough with tropical sunshine, beaches, relaxation and romance, it probably won't be necessary to give people the facts about its ingredients or manufacturing process. Their feelings might have nothing to do with facts. Similarly, feelings can be associated with experience (for example, with 'the good old days'). However, to assume that people will always predictably act on the basis of associated feelings is to assume that they react without thinking, which is not always true.

Similarity

Research suggests that people are attracted to those whom they resemble. There is evidence that they find similarity pleasing, whether it be physical, experiential, attitudinal or any other kind. On that basis, one might try to generate positive public feelings towards an organization by emphasizing similarities between it and its publics. ('We are your kind of people.') However, there are too many exceptions to this principle to make it reliable, and the exceptions sometimes create strong negative feelings. It can happen that you very much dislike someone who resembles you. Furthermore, experiments designed in the late

1960s to test this hypothesis were not able to eliminate the possibility that we search for similarities between ourselves and people whose views we respect. If that is the case, our feelings of attraction stem ultimately from an intellectual concordance and any attempt to change them would have to be made through the intellectual dimension of our attitudes.

Repetition

It has been argued that the simple repetition of a promotional message can make it pleasing. In the late 1960s this hypothesis attracted the attention of a horde of researchers who wanted to disprove it. To their astonishment they found there is some truth in it; repeating a message is sometimes all it takes to dispose people favourably. But the principle is very limited in its application. First of all, the repetition may cause us to like the message but not the product. Secondly, beyond a certain point the pleasing repetition can become irritating. It would be very risky, therefore, to believe that one can win friends for an organization simply by repeating the message that it is likeable.

It is a principle of persuasive communication directly applicable to public relations: *the intellectual and emotional dimensions of attitudes, although closely linked, are separate factors, each having its own determinants.* We like certain things about which we know very little, and we dislike some things in spite of the good things we know about them. Each person can to some degree adjust this balance in his own case but the communicator has very little control over the intellectual and emotional conflicts and compromises of those who receive his messages. His best bet is to assume that if his message is accepted intellectually it will dispose the receiver to respond also with favourable feelings. If that does not happen, he can still hope that the receiver will choose to act on what he knows rather than on how he feels. This is small comfort, but the best available. We have yet to see, however, if even full acceptance of a message will lead to predictable behaviour.

From acceptance to behaviour

Throughout a political campaign pollsters commonly ask a sample of voters the following question: 'If the election were held tomorrow, for whom would you vote?' The question assumes that, on the basis of the campaign so far people will have formed an intention to vote in a certain way. It might be assumed as well, that an intention formulated halfway through a campaign will persist until voting day unless something happens to change it, and, that on election day people will actually vote as they said they would. Each of these assumptions should be questioned, not only by political pollsters but by anyone engaged in persuasive communication—including public relations practitioners.

Do our attitudes (what we know and how we feel about a proposal) generate an intention to act in a corresponding way? Not always: many people who hear about and fear the risk of flu resolve to be vaccinated; many who hear about and fear the link between sugar and tooth decay never seriously think of reducing their sugar consumption. The intention to translate attitudes into action does not follow automatically. We are not yet talking about the act itself; we are talking only about the intention to act—the decision to perform, at some later time, a particular act. This decision is not irreversible. You can still change your mind. But clearly, unless you first have the intention you will never later perform the act. It is a necessary condition; on what does it depend?

Proposed action
First of all, one has to recognize and accept the relationship between a persuasive communication and a proposed action. A product advertisement obviously proposes that one buy the product. But to what specific course of action was the United Nations Year of Women related? For most people there was none. Many people and organizations, on their own initiative, carried out appropriate action programmes. But most did not. Nor could they have been expected to. If attitudes generated by an information campaign are to lead to visible results, people must know precisely what action is proposed and how they are to go about it. Possibly by design, but certainly in effect, most people never received this kind of information during Women's Year. The following principle of persuasive communication could well be applied to public relations practice: *the transition from a favourable attitude to an intention to act demands clear and precise direction.*

But even that may not be enough. Proposed actions can be graded according to their consequences: a proposal that you 'think about' something is not very demanding; a proposal that you write for more information on it would require greater effort; that you attend a debate would call for still more; that you join a voluntary organization more again; and finally, a proposal that you radically change your way of life would be extremely demanding. If the proposed action is too consequential, you might reverse your favourable attitude towards the whole idea. On the other hand, even feeble attitudes can motivate a resolution to perform a small, simple act. The intention to act depends on what satisfactions and difficulties are linked to the proposed action, and what values you assign to those consequences. The values might be strictly personal: given your personality, how great an effort would it cost you to attend a public meeting on the establishment of a club for homosexuals? Although values rooted in personality are relatively stable, their expression can vary with circumstances and in public relations that may be more important. A sense of insecurity can lead union members under one set of circumstances to be viciously hostile and under different circumstances to be maturely disposed to negotiate with Management. The evaluation of a proposed action might, on the other hand, be guided more by social norms: what will your friends think? your family? your neighbours? Personal and social norms sometimes pull in opposite directions. Not uncommonly office employees work amicably with people they would never accept as personal friends for reasons of social class. These considerations suggest that the decision to perform a given act can be very much influenced by social and personal circumstances.

Persistence of intention

Will an intention to act, once formed, persist over the required period of time? Sometimes the proposed action is to be performed immediately: 'Fill out this form right away and drop it in the box on the counter.' In a case like that, the persuasive communicator either wins or loses on the spot. More often there is a time lag between the proposal and the performance of the act. Immediately after a speech by Candidate X you might form the intention to vote for him, but the election is a month off. What can happen to your intention during the interval? There are four patterns.

Ideally (for Candidate X) the content of his speech will be remembered, its emotional impact will remain high, and your intention to vote for him will persist at full strength right through to election day. However, even if some of what he said is forgotten or the force of his presentation wanes a bit, what remains could still be enough to sustain your intention to vote for him. But things do not always go that well for Candidate X. Partial persistence, the second pattern, is quite common. Something about either the speech or the candidate wears off. In retrospect his logic seems tenuous, his presentation a bit forced, or changing circumstances cast doubt on the advisability of his policies. At this point although your intention to vote for Candidate X persists it is extremely vulnerable. If your retrospective views or the changed circumstances significantly alter the situation, your intention to vote for him might disintegrate altogether. This is the third pattern—non-persistence. Other things can bring it on: you might, for example, just not be a vigorous political animal and your fickle intention to vote might die a natural death before election day. Finally, there is the pattern called the Sleeper Effect. It can happen that some time after the campaign speech your intention to vote for Candidate X grows stronger. Perhaps when you heard the speech you were somewhat put off by it, but over time its negative aspects fade and you become more impressed by the logic of what was said. Remember the 'cognitive responses'—your personal internal reactions to communications? They can remain active long after the communication that stimulated them has ceased. They could, therefore, continue to propose arguments that embellish the cause of Candidate X and strengthen your intention to vote for him.

Intention to action
Assume, then, that your intention to perform a particular act (proposed in a persuasive communication) remains alive. On the day of reckoning will it translate into action? Will you actually do what you said you would? Again we must say: not automatically. You may declare, 'I'm giving no more money to charity; let the government provide for the poor.' But when a canvasser calls at your door, you donate. A university student condemns what he sees as the capitalist system of exploitation and consumerism, but after graduation he lives a bourgeois life in the suburbs. The environment in which an intention is formed is totally different from that in which an action is to be performed. Intentions are formed in a realm of concepts, stereotypes, ideals and values; behaviour takes place in a world of real people and conditions that cause real pleasure or pain. Only a very strong intention can survive in an environment of abrasive or alluring reality.

Environment also triggers habits. As soon as I arrive at my office each morning I have a cup of coffee. I can't say I need it. I may not even enjoy it much, but I invariably have one. It's the environment that does it—the time of day, my office, the fact that I have just put my briefcase on the desk and removed my coat. That early morning coffee has become a habit, and habits can offset the best of intentions.

There is nothing mysterious about all of this. These observations gain as much from commonsense and experience as from scientific research. It is surprising therefore that they are frequently overlooked in public relations practice. Admittedly not every public relations programme is meant to result in some form of action. Long-range programmes are generally designed simply to sustain favourable public dispositions, which are unquestionably important. But if the day comes when these attitudes must be expressed in action, it would be extremely risky to assume that no further work need be done, that because the public respects the organization they will support it actively. Dispositions, especially favourable ones, seldom find their own way to action. They have to be motivated and guided.

The diffusion of innovation

The primary concern of a public relations practitioner is the establishment and maintenance of good relationships between an organization and its publics. The distinction between establishment and maintenance is important because they call for different strategies. Of the two, establishing relationships is generally the more difficult since it entails the cultivation of new attitudes or at least the redirection of existing ones towards a new object, namely, the organization. In other words, it is a matter of motivating change, gaining acceptance of a new idea. People sometimes speak of ideas 'whose time has come' implying that their spread will be powered by their timeliness. Maybe there are such ideas but most, no matter how good they are, need promotion if they are to be widely accepted.

Stages of diffusion
In the jargon of communication studies, the spread of a new idea is called the 'diffusion of innovation' and it is a process that has attracted the interest of many researchers. Having analysed the psychological process which takes place in the mind of the recipient of a persuasive message, let us now examine the role of the sender of the message, the communicator trying to persuade someone to accept a new idea. As the recipient of a message processes it psychologically, the communicator does not stand idly by waiting for the final result. He remains active, adapting his strategy to each phase of the psychological process and being very careful to keep the two processes (his and the recipient's) synchronized. Thus, just as there are stages in the recipient's psychological process, there are corresponding stages in the strategy of persuasive communication. They are not clearly demarcated but researchers have identified five basic stages:

(1) Creating awareness of the new idea;
(2) Providing more information on it;
(3) Providing opportunity for evaluating the new idea;
(4) Assisting the recipient to reach a final decision;
(5) Guiding the recipient to act on his decision.

Timing the shifts from one stage to the next of his strategy is one part of the communicator's task; he must also, with each shift, choose the most appropriate form of communication to employ. Let us consider an example.

Stage 1
An organization promoting the right of women to obtain abortion on demand has set up a new office in a community where the idea has very little public acceptance. The organization's public relations officer is therefore faced with the challenge of diffusing an innovation. In Stage 1 he wants to make people aware of the organization's existence in the community and of the services it is prepared to offer interested people. He does not yet want to elaborate on these services or engage in debate on the subject, he simply wants to make people aware of the new situation. He must, then, develop a suitable message and choose appropriate communication channels. Conceivably spot announcements on radio and television would be best. Through these media he could reach practically the entire population, and a spot announcement would be enough to bring to their attention the basic information he wants them to have.

Assuming that he gains their attention with his message, the communicator knows that from that point on the recipient's cognitive responses will be in operation. These responses will probably trigger both supportive and countering arguments to the idea of abortion on demand. At this stage of the psychological process, therefore, many people may want more information on both the organization and the question of abortion. The communicator then shifts to Stage 2 of his strategy.

Stage 2
In Stage 2 he makes additional information available. Given the very personal nature of the question and its highly charged moral dimension, radio and television would probably not be appropriate channels at this stage. The communicator may feel that printed information would be more suitable—pamphlets and brochures, perhaps. People could read them privately and reread them at their leisure. The electronic media would deprive them of this opportunity. The organization should be ready to provide any type of information requested—on its own history, structure and operation as well as on every aspect of the question—technical, ethical, philosophical, moral, legal, etc.

Stage 3
Psychologically the recipient of the message might then experience some tension between his understanding of the issue and his

feelings with respect to it. If this occurs the communicator must be ready to shift to Stage 3 of his strategy, assisting the recipient to reconcile any intellectual-emotional conflict and arrive at a clear evaluation of the idea. This would almost certainly call for interpersonal communication with each interested person. The organization would have to provide facilities for private discussions between inquirers and knowledgeable consultants. As well, they would have to be prepared to supplement interpersonal communication with any other appropriate form, for example additional printed material, an audio-visual presentation, filmed or videotaped interviews with legal or medical authorities, etc. (In a different situation, for example one involving the acceptance of a new product, people would at this stage be given a chance to test the product as a further aid to evaluating it.)

Stage 4
Stage 4 is optional. In the case we are considering, people may need no more information from the organization to reach a decision for or against abortion on demand. They may need only time to mull over the question privately. But in other situations they may need further guidance towards making a decision. For example, when a Canadian provincial government had to win acceptance for new fish marketing policies, it was necessary in Stage 4 to arrange public meetings in some communities to give fishermen the chance to hear each other's views and debate with government representatives. The content of communication at this stage and the channels selected obviously depend on the situation.

Stage 5
The final stage in the diffusion of innovation relates directly to the final stage in the psychological processing of persuasive messages. We saw that if people are expected to manifest their acceptance of an idea, they must be given clear direction on what form of action they are to take. In the example we have been examining, if people have been led to accept the idea of abortion on demand, it might then be important for the organization to have them express that acceptance in some perceptible way. They may be asked, for example, to participate in a rally, or sign a petition to the government, or join the organization paying a membership fee to help finance the costs of its campaign.

It is worth repeating that the stages in the diffusion process, like those in the psychological process, are not clearly demarcated. They can, however, be discerned with enough clarity to allow the communicator to match his strategy to the changing needs of the recipient. That is important.

Channel selection

In the light of what has just been said about the process of diffusing innovation, it should be clear that in planning most public
relations projects, one does not decide on a fixed configuration of
communication channels. Rather, the project plan provides for a
continual adaptation of channels to the public's changing needs.
And in making these adaptations, planners select from a wide
variety of available channels. It would be an intimidating task to
draw up a comprehensive list of them. The following partial list is
offered merely as a point of reference:

Print Media
  Local and national newspapers
  Free distribution newspapers
  Periodicals
  House journals
  Annual reports
  Newsletters
  Direct mail
  Special booklets

Electronic Media
  Local and national radio and television
  Closed-circuit television
  Film
  Audio-visual presentations

Interpersonal Communication
  Speeches
  Meetings
  Conference telephone

Display
  Exhibitions
  Posters
  Advertising

Events
  General meetings
  Press conferences
  Open house
  Sponsorships (marathons, concerts etc)

Most textbooks offer similar lists, which are helpful if only to jar the practitioner out of his usual, routine methods of going about his job. For example, those who equate public relations with media relations should be reminded of the importance of interpersonal communication. The spoken word remains a powerful instrument of persuasion. Public speeches, committee meetings, luncheon briefings, even office visits are all potentially effective channels. Unfortunately they are often downgraded in comparison with the mass media, as though the superior effectiveness of the media could not be questioned. Neither interpersonal nor mass-media communication is absolutely effective. Their effectiveness depends on the ways in which and the purposes for which they are used. It is equally misleading to think of these two general types as mutually exclusive. There are important overlapping categories. In a press conference, for example, one directly addresses media representatives while relying on the media to carry the message further. Similarly, in radio and television interviews one often retains sufficient control over the message and its delivery to consider these situations as sharing the direct-ness of interpersonal communication. Direct-mail communication, although strictly speaking not interpersonal, offers enough creative freedom to accommodate the most personal tastes. And finally, in most cultures today media and interpersonal communication constantly interact. An alert keynote convention speaker is aware that in the minds of his listeners everything he says is supported, challenged or contradicted by what they have heard through the media.

Effectiveness and efficiency

The apparent trade-off between media and interpersonal communication is only one of several traps besetting the communications planner. Among others are: one-way communication versus two-way; spontaneous versus planned communication; organization control versus external control; large audience versus small audience, etc. In trying to work out the most advantageous compromise between these apparent trade-offs the planner can be lured by still another—effectiveness versus efficiency. Efficiency is not simply stinginess—using as few resources as possible on a project. To be efficient is to *achieve the project objectives* with the least possible expenditure of resources. Efficiency assumes effectiveness. If reaching the greatest number of people at least cost is not an effective way of communicating with them, it is not efficient either.

The most intelligent escape from this confusion is offered by a single principle: *in public relations, the preferred channel of communication is the one that most effectively reaches the public for whom a message is intended.* There must be a direct line through project objectives to identified publics to selected communication channels. Few practitioners would ignore this principle in designing a particular project, but in continuing programmes it is frequently overlooked. The urge to reach ever-larger audiences grows quietly and is justified on the grounds that the organization's basic message differs little if at all from one public to the next. Not uncommonly the continuing performance of a public relations department is evaluated by multiplying two sums—total column inches of published releases and total circulation of the publications in which they appeared. Few practitioners would ever admit to being guided by this criterion but their respect for it is reflected in their unqualified sense of accomplishment at planting a press release in a national daily newspaper. And for many who have not yet savoured the accomplishment it is a recurring dream. It therefore deserves to be analysed with seriousness.

The purpose of the news media
Any fruitful discussion of the merits of sending a press release to a newspaper has to take into account the purpose of the organization responsible for the release and that of the newspaper to which it is sent. In times when people lived in small, relatively isolated villages, they knew a lot more about each other than we and our fellow citizens do. And they knew more about their community than we do about ours—the general health of the people, the conditions of public facilities, the quality of education, the practice of religion, and the ways in which community members interacted socially. But they knew very little about other such villages, still less about the rest of the country, and almost nothing about what was going on in the rest of the world. Gradually though, over a period of centuries things changed: many people moved from one village to another, some travelled to other parts of the country, and some even migrated to other parts of the world. A number of factors contributed to that change, among them, increased populations, better communication and transport systems and the lure of greener pastures. People thus got to know more about what was happening elsewhere and the more they knew the more they wanted to know.

Still later, through things like international trade and commerce, tourism and the potential international impact of developments in individual countries, people's thirst for information became insatiable. And their need for it increased as their lives became increasingly affected by events in the rest of the world. But the problem of tracking down the information they needed and wanted was formidable—enter the mass media.

It is not as though the media came into existence just at the critical stage of this problem; they evolved with the problem, becoming increasingly sophisticated as public need became more pressing. And one should not be persuaded by the problematic historical context to think of the media in purely altruistic terms, as though they exist exclusively for the public good. Nevertheless, public service is and has always been a key element in the policy of any media system. In effect, the media say to the public: 'Listen, we understand your problem. We know the kind of information you need and want, and we have the personnel and facilities to track it down anywhere in the world and deliver it to you. Just leave it to us.' On the basis of that reassuring pledge they have encircled the earth with satellite and terrestrial communication systems which transmit the reports of thousands of journalists from every corner of the world into our living rooms. This description of the media's function, by the way, is based on the 1957 Westley and MacLean model of mass communication (see Westley B and MacLean M, A Conceptual Model for Communication Research in *Journalism Quarterly*, 34, 1957, pp.31-8). Importantly, each individual mass medium to some degree shares this view of its function.

To repeat, the media are not motivated by pure altruism as if they were selflessly relieving the pain of a legitimate public addiction. There is money to be made in providing the kind of public service just described. The more people you serve the more money you make; and the more helpful information you provide, the more people you are likely to serve. The media therefore have both financial and social reasons for ever increasing their audiences and satisfying them with information they need or simply find interesting. And the national daily newspaper to which the public relations practitioner sends his news release is one such medium.

The purpose of the news release
Why does he send it? Obviously not simply to satisfy the same public needs and interests that occupy the media. The public relations practitioner works for an organization whose interests have a staked claim on his concern. When he sends a release to a newspaper he naturally hopes that his organization will benefit from it. That is essential to his function. He is not indifferent to the needs of the general public, and he certainly should never work against them. In fact he tries to identify his organization's need with that of the general public. But here we touch on a fundamental problem. In working with a newspaper the public relations practitioner is not in direct contact with the general public.

He is dealing with an institution which has, to its own satisfaction, interpreted public need and interest. If the practitioner wants to reach the general public through the newspaper he must present his material in a way that reflects *that newspaper's* interpretation of public interest. Otherwise his material will be rejected as unsuited to the paper's editorial policies.

There are, therefore, four elements in the situation: the actual public need; the newspaper's interpretation of public need; the organization's need; and the organization's interpretation of public need. If all four were perfectly aligned there would be no problem. The newspaper would recognize the organization's view of public need as valid and corresponding to its own, and it would see the organization's specific need as positively related to that shared perception of public need. The organization's press release would then be publishable (subject only to available space and the priorities of competing unsolicited material). Unfortunately the organization's concept of public need does not always correspond to that of the newspaper. Therefore when the practitioner declares that his organization's need reflects that of the general public, he might find that the newspaper disagrees. Furthermore, he may be thwarted by the newspaper's suspicion that public relations practitioners simply want to exploit for their own limited interests, the paper's access to the general public.

Conflicting interests
Is there any way to resolve the sometimes conflicting interests of the newspaper and public relations? Could they not both take a fresh look at public need and decide which of them has best interpreted it? Conceivably they could, but it is not likely they would ever agree to such a joint undertaking. Besides, genuine universal public need is very hard to recognize. It is more practical to conceive of it as the ensemble of particular needs of individual publics. The public relations practitioner, of all people, should appreciate this: it is the standard public relations approach. It is also, by the way, the policy of most media. As a rule, each medium defines for itself the specific publics it wants to serve. No medium can satisfy everyone. Even the mass circulation daily newspapers, which may appear to address themselves to everyone, have their priorities. Some concentrate more than others on national news over international, politics over the environment, financial news over entertainment, sports over science, White middle-class interests over those of minorities. Nevertheless, certain of the national dailies seem to provide a sufficiently diverse coverage to attract the attention of most of the publics important to any public relations practitioner. Would it not be worth-

while, in the interests of efficiency, to send a release to one of them? Under one condition yes—when the subject matter of the release is unquestionably of significant public interest as defined by that newspaper. Only then can you be reasonably sure that publication of the release will truly serve your purpose. If the item does tie in with the editor's view of public interest but is of only modest significance, efficiency cannot clearly justify the selection of a national newspaper as an appropriate channel. It would amount to a dilution of the information needed by each of your publics into a concoction you hope will satisfy them all. The effect would be too diffuse to be clearly detected and too slight to be confidently measured.

Bad publicity—good publicity

The temptation to blitz the media (especially the press), ignoring interpretations of public need and the special interests of special publics, is particularly strong in times of crisis. A barrage of positive publicity seems to some planners to be the only surefire response to an attack of bad publicity. Here, for example, is a statement by an Area Officer of Social Services: 'The man on the street still does not know what we do except via periodic chunks of largely negative publicity, usually in respect of child care.' As an antidote he proposed 'a proactive, positive approach to advertising the services they (the social service departments) have developed...' Over the past few years the same essential plea has been voiced by administrative officers of the police department: 'Police officers are being unjustly accused of violence, prejudice and criminal negligence. It's time we publicized the good things they do, the day-in day-out acts of courage and dedication that go unnoticed.' These calls for more favourable publicity are not usually directed to anyone who can do anything about them, but once in a while a public relations practitioner receives the mandate directly and is expected to act on it. Among my own associates, the public relations officer of a hospital received such an instruction following the death of a patient as a result of professional malpractice. Unfortunately, in the administrative confusion that followed the death the public relations officer was not able to convince his superiors that the antidote would have no effect. In each of the three cases just cited it is almost unthinkable that good publicity could offset the bad. The good things people do are not evaluated by the same criteria as the bad.

Criteria for evaluating acts
Consider the criteria: obviously the nature of an act bears on the

evaluation of its performance and that nature does not change with the agent. Murder is murder whether committed by a nun or a Mafia mobster. And if both of them perform a kindness the act is not defined differently in each case. But the public merit of an act, the public estimation of its final goodness or badness, depends very much on who performs it and on who is affected by it. If a good act is performed by someone who is expected to perform it we don't assign any special merit to it. A policeman is supposed to prevent crime and when one of them does so we simply say (albeit with gratitude), 'He was just doing his job.' If a civilian does the same thing he is praised, maybe even rewarded. Similarly if a notorious criminal is caught behaving illegally we disapprove but without the shocked abhorence we might express if we heard of a magistrate doing the same thing.

As well, our appraisal of an act depends very much on the person affected by it. A good act performed for someone who needs it (helping the handicapped) is regarded more favourably than the same act done for someone who might very well have done it himself. And an evil act is considered worse if the person affected commands special respect or sympathy. Crimes against children evoke a unique horror, and those committed against royalty or statesmen are sometimes punished more severely than the same acts committed against ordinary people.

Whether these evaluative criteria are altogether reasonable is not the question, they are publicly accepted (at least in our culture) and that is what counts. Therefore, the hospital which had suffered the misfortune of a patient death through surgical malpractice could not reasonably hope that the negative publicity triggered by the event would be offset by public reminders that the overwhelming majority of operations carried out in the hospital were successful. People expect operations performed in a hospital to be successful. They approve, certainly, but their favourable evaluation is in no way special. On the contrary, their negative evaluation of an unnecessary death would be very heavily weighted by the fact that it occurred through malpractice in a hospital. The negative would simply outweigh the positive and a frantic effort to 'improve media relations' would do nothing to change that. To be sure, a public information programme would be essential. But a flurry of smiling press releases might very well give the impression of a whitewash. It would be more to the point to assure the public that the incident would be thoroughly investigated and any criminal culpability would be treated according to law.

Periodic bad publicity
In the long term a responsive public information programme

would have a different purpose. A continuous record of commendable performance over a prolonged period might, if publicized, obliterate the memory of a tragic event. However, this remedy seems unfortunately beyond the reach of some public services. They are not able to build up an impressively long unbroken record of positive service. Sporadically, things go wrong; it seems inevitable, the result of human weakness and difficult circumstances. The police force, for example, can never hope to avoid all the physical confrontations that sometimes bring on them accusations of violence. Probably too they cannot hope to entirely eliminate the shady behaviour of some police officers. In other words, they have to expect that periodically they will be hit with bad publicity. In those moments of crisis the bad news will not be offset by a spate of publicity about unsung heroes, but its damage may well be limited if it is seen against a background of persistent honest effort. The police force will seldom get extra marks for being good, but if it is known that they try always to be good they will lose fewer marks when they are caught being bad. That is the purpose of a continuing positive information programme.

To return to the Area Officer quoted at the beginning of this chapter: he wisely recommended that in advance of his proposed advertising campaign a careful inventory of social service resources and a re-examination of service priorities be carried out. Based on these preliminaries the campaign, he felt, would not stimulate an unmanageable demand for services. This was a sound recommendation. A close correspondence between services advertised and services available would in the long run certainly contribute to a positive public evaluation of the department. His proposal exemplified an important principle: *a continuing public information programme is always linked to sound performance*, otherwise it is nothing more than misleading advertising fuelling a latent resentment that will explode the next time a public scandal provides opportunity.

Limited media power
An episode of bad publicity is invariably painful and difficult to handle, but an experienced public relations practitioner never lets himself be drawn into someone else's panic over it. It is a time to be realistic and keep one's head, to remember among other things that bad publicity does not always result in a bad image. The media are not that powerful. It was once thought they were; it was once thought that the public was unable to resist their persuasive power. Our friend the Area Officer seems to think so still: 'We all know,' he said, 'that most of us without entrenched prejudice have our opinions shaped by the information we receive.'

Since he submitted this comment in defence of his proposed media campaign it seems that by 'information' he meant 'media information'. But our opinions are shaped by an enormous number and variety of factors—the media, yes, but also the dispositions we inherit, our environment (geographic, cultural, social etc), our experience, our hopes and fears, our beliefs and ideals, probably even our blood-sugar level. The embarrassing failure of some of the most high-powered, highly sophisticated media promotion campaigns has clearly demonstrated the limited potential of the media. Cigarettes have survived a media onslaught for years—not a flattering comparison for public services but evidence that satisfaction can outweigh negative publicity in an evaluation.

Political criteria

Something else to remember: sometimes the administrators of public services are more disturbed by bad media coverage than is the general public. Their fear is that negative reports might move higher-level authorities (politicians) to short-circuit programmes or cut budgets. After all, public dissatisfaction could translate into a loss of votes. A politician hypersensitive to this possibility might therefore demonstrate his 'sense of public responsibility' by taking action against a department floundering in what looks to him like a storm of public opprobrium. This is not to belittle the problem, just to suggest a different perspective.

Special events

The special event may be a single element in a project that includes others, or it may be a project in its own right. In either case it invariably combines several forms of communication. It is generally an occasion to meet people, therefore interpersonal communication figures prominently. Usually it is also a time to distribute printed materials and possibly to mount a display which might include audio-visual presentations. Depending on the nature and significance of the event, it might become subject matter for news releases and perhaps even for some media coverage.

In public relations, 'special event' is a catch-all term which refers to a variety of functions. Some, like press conferences, take place periodically; others may be annual events—the open house, the annual general meeting, and certain formal ceremonies like graduations; still others are staged exceptionally—concerts, exhibitions, sports days and the like. The diversity of special events makes it difficult to find a common denominator, but it

seems safe to say that they all include an element of public participation. In any case, it is in that sense that the term is used here.
People attend a special event, usually by invitation, and it is
hoped they will participate in it.

Attendance versus participation

The distinction between participating in an event and simply
attending it is important. To say that one hopes the public will
participate implies that if they do not the event will in some way
be incomplete. The public is expected to be active, to play a role in
it. Clearly then, the event is not entirely in the hands of the organization. It is a shared happening in which both the organization
and the public have roles to play. Textbook treatments of special
events almost invariably include checklists of things to be done
in preparation. These are helpful, even necessary, but they could
create the false impression that if everything on the list is taken
care of in advance the event will be fully under control; that is not
so. The checklist gives that impression because it covers only
those things which are within the organization's control. It does
not, cannot, include the specifics of public participation. How the
public will behave at an event remains an unknown factor. Yet
the event is, in its very essence, the common product of the
organization and its public.

Let us call the event as designed by the organization the 'skeleton event' and distinguish it from the 'complete event' which is
what actually takes place. The skeleton event includes all the
details that identify it as being of a certain type. The specifics of a
press conference, for example, obviously differ from those of an
open house. These differentiating details are what are protected
by checklists. They are taken very seriously because if the 'skeleton' is weak or deformed the actual event will necessarily be
sickly. However, a skeleton is an incomplete entity. It is designed
to support other elements. In the case of the special event, what
supplementary elements must the skeleton be able to support?
There are two kinds: necessary elements and possible elements.

Necessary elements

First the necessary elements: in an annual general meeting, the
format naturally includes time for the discussion of questions
from the floor. However, the planners cannot be certain there will
be any questions. They cannot themselves legitimately supply
questioners. Questions are required from the public to complete
the event; they are a necessary supplement to the question period included in the skeleton event. A stony silence from those
attending the meeting would have to be interpreted by the organization with some uneasiness. Another example: at an open house

provision is generally made for guided tours; if the visitors showed no interest in taking the tours the event would lack something essential to its purpose. But again, the organizers cannot guarantee that the open house will be attended by a respectable number of people interested in guided tours. That element must be provided by the public.

Possible elements
The second type of element missing from the skeleton cannot be called necessary, but only possible. The participants in an event might (but need not) contribute to it in a variety of unforeseen ways. Although unforeseen, these elements invariably enrich the event; they don't attach themselves to it like leeches. If in the open house just mentioned an impressive number of people took the guided tours, they would of course react to what they saw. The organizers may hope their impressions would all be favourable but they cannot be sure of that. Visitors may be bored, confused, perhaps even put off. However, any reaction would contribute to the event, even negative reactions, by enriching the communication between the organization and its publics. In this sense the event is, as we have said, the common product of both the organization and its publics.

Notice, however, that possible responses can differ from one participant to another. While some may be favourably impressed by what they see at an open house, others might be disturbed or irritated. On what will these differences depend? The event itself may have something to do with it. Certain people are suspicious of annual meetings, for example. They expect a whitewashing of the organization and nothing can fully set them at ease. Then too, the conditions in which the event is held can trigger various responses. A voluntary organization that holds its annual general meeting in a conference room of a luxurious hotel might encounter a range of responses—from those impressed by the organization's apparent financial health, to those angered by the expenditure that apparently went into the meeting. The dispositions of individual participants will also explain various reactions. At any general meeting there are some experienced participants who interpret everything in the light of what they have seen and heard before. Usually too there are a few newcomers prepared to accept everything with an open mind. Others may have come out of curiosity, loyalty, animosity, or simply to accompany a friend.

Each person who attends a special event, therefore, will effectively participate in a different event. Only the planned skeleton event will be identical for all of them. Necessary elements will be contributed by some participants but not by others, and possible responses (participants' impressions), being very personal will differ from one to another.

Evaluating special events

How then can the event be evaluated? All three elements have to be evaluated separately — the skeleton event; the degree to which people contributed necessary elements; and the strength and quality of their spontaneous reactions. We will discuss evaluation at length in Chapter 5; it is mentioned here to provide setting for the following principle: *in planning a public relations project one structures it with an eye to later evaluation.* Evaluating the skeleton event is fairly straightforward. The checklist used in preparing for the event serves as a guide in assessing the adequacy of its structure and organization. But even if the skeleton was perfect, the event would have to be chalked up as a failure if those who attended failed to participate. The skeleton, after all, was designed only to make participation possible. The degree of participation is therefore a key factor in the evaluation. The third factor, the impressions of participants, is also important but cannot be measured with precision. Since there are several ways to sound these impressions it is specified in the project plan which method will later be used.

Symbols

The point was made earlier that a special event comprises many forms of communication — multiple channels and a variety of messages. Frequently too, it includes a number of different activities. This diversity may at times be exciting but it must be prevented from disintegrating into a confusion of isolated elements. Planners generally achieve this through the use of strong unifying symbols, ideally one single symbol. It may be an emblem, a slogan, a person, an accomplishment, a goal — something which orients all the messages and activities, giving the event cohesiveness.

Symbols are important in public relations because just as they can pull together the elements of a special event they can do the same for any other project and indeed for a continuing public relations programme. But they must be selected and handled with extreme care, as the following anecdote illustrates.

It was a hot, dry summer in England. Not much for kids to do during the summer holidays, in the industrial towns of the West Midlands. But relief from the boredom if not from the heat did come to one town, in the form of a sports day organized by the combined youth associations and sponsored principally by a major soft drink firm. There were track and field events, a volleyball tournament, a bicycle race, an exhibition of children's art, and an amateur talent contest.

Up to a point just before things went horribly wrong, how could one most simply describe what the sponsoring soft drink firm was doing? Any one of the participating young people might have said, 'They're just giving us a good time. There's nothing much to do here in the summer and this is fun.' With slightly more perception the child's parents might have said, 'They're buying goodwill. People appreciate it when you do something for kids.' There is no attempt in either of these answers to go beneath the surface. On the face of it the soft drink company was simply doing something for young people and hoping it would be appreciated: public relations.

Late in the afternoon, while the amateur contest was going on, a scuffle broke out at the canteen. No alcohol was served but some of the young people were drunk; they must have brought their own. Perhaps too, some were on drugs. In any case the fight sparked an ugly mood that spread into the crowd, igniting other scuffles. Soon there was a small riot. Bottles and glasses were smashed, furniture was overturned and the first of the injured were helped away. By the time the police arrived the canteen was a shambles, half a dozen people had been injured including two who had been stabbed. The day ended in sadness and frustration.

The following day the town council's director of sports and recreation held a press conference. Seated at a table he was flanked by the directors of the various youth associations and representatives of the sponsoring organizations, most conspicuously the soft drink firm. By their presence they endorsed the public statement, and a tough statement it was. The sports director denounced the 'irresponsible hooligans' who had 'disgraced the community' and he assured the town's 'decent' people that everything possible would be done to make the offenders realize that 'savagery' would not be tolerated in this town.

What must now be said about the position of the soft drink firm? Had it changed? Previously the company had presented itself as a friend of young people, now it endorsed a statement denouncing some of them as 'irresponsible hooligans'. The young people, as a segment of the town's population, had not changed. Before, during and after the sports day that portion of the population included young people of every hue—creative, lazy, generous, bored, courteous, violent, whatever. Clearly, in promoting the interests of young people, the company had harboured unexpressed reservations. They had not sided with youth simply as people of a certain age; the violent ones were the same age. The company had associated itself with young people as symbols—symbols of hope, integrity, promise. And when certain young people showed themselves not to be such symbols, the company dissociated itself from them.

Reality and symbols

There is a difference between reality and symbols of reality. There are further differences in the ways people interpret and re-act to symbols. The reality in this case was the town's future, its development, its prosperity, its endurance as a community of law-abiding citizens. The soft drink firm had taken young people as a symbol of that. It associated itself with them to show that it shared the community's hopes and wanted to contribute to its future. Did it make a wise choice in selecting the young as a sym-bol of promise? Certainly it chose a familiar symbol. But the interpretation of symbols can change over time, it can change from one culture to another, even from one individual to another. In other words it depends on the circumstances and experience of the person interpreting the symbol. Probably there were people in that English town who had already had unpleasant experi-ences with young people. For them, the young might long ago have become a symbol of alienation and trouble, and the com-pany's association with them would have been taken negatively from the start. The way people interpret a symbol is more import-ant in communication than the actual link between the symbol and the reality it is supposed to represent. Whether young people *in fact* symbolize hope matters less than whether they are pub-licly accepted as symbols of hope. We communicate with sym-bols (written words, gestures, sounds, emblems etc); the realities they are supposed to represent constitute another world.

Semiotics

In the science that deals with this (semiotics) a *symbol* is one of three types of sign: the other two are *index* and *icon*. An index is a sign directly linked with its object. Smoke is an index of fire. There is no problem in interpreting these signs. Their link with reality is factual. An icon resembles its object in some way. A photograph is an icon resembling what was photographed. The word 'meow' is iconic, resembling the sound a cat makes. The link between an icon and its object is not as close as in the case of an index so the possibility of misinterpretation is greater. Still, icons don't create many problems. They are not generally contro-versial and mistakes can be cleared up. The problems arise, as we have seen, with the third type of sign—the symbol.

The link between a symbol and reality is arbitrary. It is estab-lished either by rule or agreement. A red traffic light means

STOP, by rule. There is no inherent relationship between a red light and the command to stop. The shape 2 stands for a pair of objects simply because we have agreed that it should. Again, there is nothing inherent in the relationship. But agreements can vary in strength. The agreement that the shape 2 should represent a pair of things is strong, but how strong is the agreement that the number 13 is unlucky? What does long hair on a man symbolize?—rebellious unorthodoxy, artistic sensibility, genius, poverty? There is some agreement on each of these interpretations but not enough on any one of them to make the symbol effective. Obviously the weaker the public agreement the greater the risk of a breakdown in communication. If there is no public agreement a symbol becomes purely personal and cannot be used in communication. If a crow should fly through my open window I might take it as a sign that the world is about to end, but not many people would share that interpretation. Company trademarks are often symbols—arbitrary graphic designs with no essential link to the qualities they are meant to stand for. The company then tries through its performance to establish a link in the public mind between the symbol and the reality.

Agreement on symbolic meaning
Let's return to the sports day in England. Youth was not the only symbol of interest; sport was another. The soft drink firm chose to sponsor a sports day, not a motor rally. Sport symbolizes among other things fair play, physical fitness (which in turn might symbolize moral uprightness), respectable aggressiveness, perseverance. There is no consensus on this symbolism; some people might think of sport as symbolizing hateful competitiveness. Still, there is probably enough agreement on the respectability of sport to make the sponsorship of a sports day a safe choice.

And what agreement is there on the symbolism of youth? The interpretation of young people as a symbol has, over a period of centuries, undergone a significant evolution in Britain. There was a time when they were looked upon with very little respect. They constituted a body of cheap, unskilled, available labour, to some employers, nothing more. Only much later, when they had come to symbolize hope and prosperity, were people proud to say that the country belonged to its youth. Today the fear of unemployment has sapped their confidence. Many are dejected, some are desperate. It is not for them to decide what they symbolize. It is not even important that they symbolize anything. But the soft drink firm assumed they symbolized something and chose to act on that assumption. It is not clear, however, that before acting the company observed two very important principles:

(1) *In using symbols in public relations, one assesses the degree to which one's interpretation of them is shared;*
(2) *In using symbols in public relations, one makes sure that the symbolism is reasonably stable, not shifting towards significant change.*

The Action Plan

Following the statement of final and intermediate objectives and the logical links between them, the plan presents a detailed description of precisely how the project is to be carried out. This description is called the Action Plan and it includes three things:

(1) A description of all activities to be performed in carrying out the project;
(2) The phasing and scheduling of these activities;
(3) A description of the system by which the project is to be managed.

The guiding principle is that *the Action Plan spells out in concrete terms the requirements and implications of everything the rest of the plan proposes in ideal terms.* For example, project objectives might previously have been discussed in terms of expectations; in the Action Plan the factual bases for those expectations are made clear. It answers questions like: who is going to do what; how; over what period of time; using what resources?

Description of activities

The trick in developing this section of the plan is to provide enough information to fully support the proposed project, but not so much that the plan becomes an indecipherable mass of detail. How much detail is too much? It depends on who has to approve the plan. Those who pass final judgement generally consider two things separately—but not independently: the substance of the proposal and its cost. The substance includes the nature of the project, its final and intermediate objectives, its scheduling and phasing and the personnel, materials and facilities needed to carry it out. The cost includes the amount of money needed to pay for each element of the plan, the sources of funds, and the financing arrangements. Obviously the plan's substance and its cost are closely linked: the substance justifies the cost, and the cost very much affects the feasibility of the substance.

It can happen, though, that two (sometimes even three) different authorities must pass judgement on the plan. Certainly in-house Management will have to appraise it. But if an external consultant has assisted in the planning (or has been fully responsible for it) the Management of his agency will also want to approve it before submitting it to the client-organization. Sometimes a third organization is to be asked to fund the project, for example, a government department or a private funding agency. In that case the Management of the funding organization will also have to approve the proposal. The amount of detail to be included in the Project Document depends on how much each involved organization knows about the client-organization. One does not belabour things they already know, but certain known facts may have to be emphasized — perhaps certain organization policies or traditions. And one never makes unwarranted assumptions. For example, while an external agency might be aware of the client-organization's resources it might not know which ones are available for the project. If all the necessary resources are not available in the client-organization, where are additional resources going to come from? It might be necessary, for example, to hire part-time help; if so, that must be made clear in the project proposal.

In developing the Action Plan, planners are guided by their vision of the sequence of activities that will have to be performed in carrying out the project. They describe these activities clearly and, to the degree that it is necessary, they add the details that demonstrate their feasibility and assure that they will indeed be performed.

Phasing and scheduling

Over the duration of a project the achievement of certain objectives might depend on the attainment of previous ones. In the Diffusion of Innovation (previously discussed) the second stage — providing detailed information — could not be implemented before people had become aware of the new idea being proposed to them. The example we considered was that of an organization opening a new office to promote abortion on demand. If it planned to operate an information centre where people might discuss the question in detail and in privacy, it would first have to make the public aware of its existence in the community. The second stage would therefore be phased in some time after the first stage had been implemented. The first stage might then be phased out, unless it seemed preferable to continue it through all subsequent stages.

Phasing is a matter of timing, and timing is never arbitrary. It is a strategy. It must therefore have solid, logical justifications. Frequently too, it must be flexible. If a second phase depends on the completion of a previous one, the plan must be able to accommodate unforeseen delays in phase one. At the same time, the plan must be relatively firm. Delays inevitably add to costs. Planners therefore schedule each phase; that is, they indicate as precisely as possible the date on which it is to begin and its expected completion date. The implementation of complex projects with many overlapping phases is usually illustrated in a flow chart.

Project management

Even a carefully planned project can go wrong if its implementation is not well managed. All team members must know their duties, the scope of their decision-making authority and the procedures by which they are to operate. On a project carried out by a relatively small in-house team, there are generally few problems. The team members know each other and they know the organization's policies and operational systems. Difficulties are more likely on multi-phased projects involving external consultants and subcontractors. Nevertheless, the requirements for effective project management remain the same. There are four:

(1) Clear organization;
(2) Clear job descriptions;
(3) Clear policy statements;
(4) Clear systems descriptions.

(1) Clear organization
Jobs are what have to be organized, not people. Job holders may change but the jobs themselves remain until their objectives have been achieved. Some last through the duration of a project, others may be phased out according to plan. The organization is generally illustrated in a structural diagram of boxes joined by lines. Each box represents a job and the lines represent the relationships between the various job holders. Upward lines represent channels of accountability (lower-level job holders reporting to those at higher levels) and downward lines represent channels of authority (those at the top having authority exercised or delegated in various ways to those at lower levels). In either direction the lines represent channels of communication.

Structural diagrams are especially helpful on limited-term projects involving outside contracts. People who are not employed by the client-organization do not have time to learn the system by working with it for a while; they have to contribute fully to the project right from the beginning. Indeed, on some projects special structural arrangements are necessary, and even members of the in-house team may find themselves working under a system they are not used to. The important thing is that each person should clearly understand how all team members relate to each other. A public relations consultant employed by an agency while on a project contract to a client-organization has the delicate job of responding to two bosses: in his agency he might report to an Account Director who might in turn be responsible to a Board Director; in the client-organization he will generally report to Management directly, but sometimes does so through a Project Director.

Although the structural diagram will position all team members in a chain of command, each one is not simply expected to blindly take orders from the one higher. Rather, he himself will have authority to make certain decisions, as will those who report to him. In other words, each position is characterized by a set of duties and a scope of authority. The duties are those things the job holder is required to do by order or by established procedures. The authority is the decision-making power he has in carrying out his duties. For example, a photographer might be contracted to produce a set of photographs for a display. His principal duty is to deliver acceptable photographs on time. But he has the authority to decide how best to meet that requirement. He will have to make certain artistic judgements with respect to the composition of the photos, lighting, enlarging, cropping etc. He may also have authority to order equipment and supplies, and may have to supervise the work of lower-level staff working for him. He has no choice about his duties, but his authority gives him scope for initiative in fulfilling them.

In any chain of command one's authority can never infringe on that of a superior. But authority is not so restricted with respect to inferiors. In other words, decision makers have authority that can override that of lower-level people. They may seldom exercise this veto power, but it always exists. The distinction is sometimes made between immediate command and extended command. Immediate command is exercised on those who are directly subject to one's authority. Extended command reaches to those two or more steps lower on the ladder of authority. Take an example. If X is self-employed and works alone he is free to do his job any way he pleases; he answers to no-one and has authority over no-one. If he later employs Y he will give Y certain duties and will delegate to him a restricted authority to make decisions whenever he feels it necessary. If still later, Z is employed to work under Y's authority, Z too will have a set of duties and limited authority. But Z's authority will be subject to that of both Y and X. The boss, X, will have immediate command over Y and extended command over Z or any number of Zs. The situation is illustrated below.

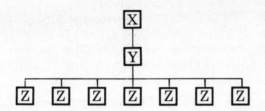

Thus workers are subject to supervisors who are responsible to middle-level managers who respond to senior managers who answer to the chief executive who may be directly subject to the president. At the upper end of such chains, authority becomes greater and absolute duties become fewer; at the lower end it is the reverse—more fixed duties and less authority.

An organization chart may reveal that certain job holders have too much authority. Too many subordinates answer to them. The result of the overload will be a breakdown in communication and decision making. On the other hand, an organization chart may not reveal that an office holder has too little authority; that situation would become evident in an examination of both his position in the organization and his job description. It could be that a job holder has been assigned responsibilities without corresponding authority. He may have inadequate control over the personnel or resources he needs to do his job. Perhaps he cannot adjust the workloads of his staff, or provide them with equipment that would assure the quality performance for which he is ultimately responsible. Clearly this is intolerable. Those boundaries of one's authority which are set by higher authority may be negotiable, but those set by the organization's established policies, structures or resources are generally more stable—not always unchangeable, though.

If, on a project, the structure of authority is not clear to team members at all levels there can be great inefficiencies. People unsure of the scope of their authority can waste a lot of time seeking approval for decisions they could make themselves, or rectifying the consequences of rescinded decisions.

(2) Clear job descriptions
A good job description specifies four things:

(a) The duties the job holder is to perform: these are the things he is directly responsible for. He cannot delegate responsibility for them; they are assigned to the position he holds. If they are not done he can be accused of having failed in his job.

(b) The people over whom he has authority and who must therefore report to him, and the resources (budget, equipment and materials) for which he is responsible.

(c) The scope of his decision-making authority: the document must specify those things that are left to the job holder's own judgement in carrying out his assigned duties.

(d) The limits set to his authority by higher authority and by organization policy, structure and resources.

To the degree that it is helpful these four things are made known not only to the job holder but to all other team members so that each one knows what the others are to do. Co-ordination is thereby better assured.

To some degree a job description is a restrictive statement, but unless it is unduly so it defines the parameters of the job holder's freedom. He would have less freedom without them because he would not know where higher authority ceases to apply directly.

On projects of short duration it is generally not necessary to reappraise job descriptions during the project implementation, but on long-term projects and continuing programmes they are re-examined regularly and updated when necessary.

(3) Clear policy statements

Policies are rules made by Management to protect the organization's best interests and to assure smooth operation, co-ordination and efficiency. Some policies are absolute, for example safety standards, maintenance procedures, security arrangements, quality control; others admit of varying degrees of flexibility—those relating to the organization's fundamental objectives being relatively stable, those depending on circumstances being less so. Needless to say, all policies must be adequately promulgated and updated whenever necessary.

(4) Clear systems descriptions

Systems are established as control mechanisms—for example, purchasing systems, communication systems, maintenance systems, requisition systems, etc. They contribute to smooth operation but they also reinforce accountability. Responsibility can be traced through systems to discover points of weakness or breakdown. Systems often have many stages; frequently therefore, they are illustrated in flow charts as phased projects are.

Costing

The purpose of keeping an eye on costs is not just to know how much money remains in the kitty at any given moment; one studies costs in order to compare them to benefits. It is that comparison that reveals whether money is being well spent. In a simple business like mowing lawns both costs and benefits may be relatively fixed. But in public relations a great number and variety of costs have to be compared to a complexity of benefits which are not always fixed and are frequently very difficult to measure. Ideally, planners would operate on the following principle: *Both in projects and continuing programmes public relations budgeting is based on cost-benefit analysis.* But this is almost always an ideal beyond reach. Still, it is worth striving for. The pursuit of the ideal provides the best available basis for sound financial planning.

Cost-effectiveness, cost-efficiency, cost-benefit

Three terms are commonly used in the literature on costing: cost-effectiveness, cost-efficiency, and cost-benefit. A project is effective if it achieves the results it is meant to achieve, in other words if it attains its objectives. If that is accomplished within the limits of the budget set for the project, one can say that the money was spent effectively. The effect is considered worth the price paid and additional expenditure would not enhance the effect. Evaluated strictly by cost-effectiveness the project was successful. On the other hand, if when the money ran out the project objectives had not been fully attained, the project was not cost-effective; quite simply, the cost did not fully achieve the desired effects. Efficiency has to do with wastefulness. An efficiently executed project is one on which no resources are unnecessarily spent. Assuming you achieve the results you hoped for, could you have done so at less expense? If so, then analysed strictly on the basis of cost-efficiency the project was not fully successful. It can happen, though, that you achieve your objectives with the least possible expenditure of resources yet the final benefit of the project is offset by unforeseen disadvantages. In that case, measured strictly by cost-benefit analysis the project could not be considered an unqualified success. Consider an example (admittedly not a typical public relations problem). A government decides to build a number of nuclear-energy plants. After lengthy negotiations contracts are awarded and the plants constructed. If the plants were constructed within the budget allocated and they work well, the project was cost-effective; if they were built with no unnecessary expenditure, the project was cost-efficient; but if public reaction is strongly negative, the project might not be cost-beneficial. Embittered public attitudes might offset the advantages of the new energy supply.

Measurement difficulties

Disadvantages are in fact costs. The problem is that they cannot always be measured as precisely as financial costs and cannot therefore be neatly entered into cost-benefit analysis. An organization might reduce its output of public information pamphlets thus achieving measurable financial savings, but the consequent change in public awareness is not precisely measurable as a cost. Risks are another type of cost difficult to measure. A company might contract with a television star for public relations purposes, but what will be the effect on the company's image if the star is involved in a scandal? Neither the likelihood nor the cost of that disadvantage can be measured.

Just as all costs cannot be precisely measured, neither can all benefits. Most notably the fundamental benefit of all public relations activity—public acceptance of an organization—cannot be measured accurately. To the degree that it reveals itself in behaviour it can be observed and measured, but behaviour is never a clear reflection of attitude. In Chapter 1 we referred to the constraint imposed on public relations by too strong a link to the quantitative types of analysis generally preferred by Management. This constraint is never more noticeable than in costing public relations programmes against their expected benefits. Neither all of the costs nor all of the benefits are quantitative.

Costing public relations

With that precaution in mind, what can be said about public relations costing? One must first of all distinguish project costs from recurrent costs. Many recurrent costs are departmental costs, for example the costs of office rental, equipment maintenance, standard services (telephone, telex etc), heating, electricity and other necessary expenses. Strictly speaking a proportion of these should be assigned to each project but this is seldom done. They remain hidden project costs. Similarly, certain public relations activities are inevitably carried out to some degree by other departments—sales or marketing, for example. In fact, one might argue that all organization activities have a public relations dimension. A secretary receiving a telephone call, the president attending a luncheon, even a truck driver delivering goods— they all make some contribution (positive or negative) to the organization's relationships with its publics. But again, the cost of these contributions is hidden.

The known and measurable costs both of projects and continuing programmes are generally of four types: labour, facilities, materials and out-of-pocket expenses. Labour costs include not only the salaries of employees but also consultants' fees. Facilities include additional equipment needed for a project (for example, extra typewriters, desks, video-display terminals etc) as well as permanently installed equipment. Materials are things that are consumed in being used, supplies of which must then be replenished—for example, office supplies. Finally, out-of-pocket costs cover things like travel, accommodation, entertainment, etc.

Cost estimates

Grouping costs into four neat categories, as we have just done, might misleadingly suggest that costing is a fairly straightforward exercise. The budget allocated for a project or a continuing programme is based on total-cost estimates; and total cost is simply the sum of the detailed costs in each of the four categories. The difficulty is in trying to match detailed expenditures to the cost estimates on which the budget was based. Detailed costs can include a formidable list of items—construction costs, media costs, travel expenses, research fees, publication costs, audiovisual production costs, speakers' fees, and the costs of conferences, meetings, banquets, exhibitions etc—all of these broken down into countless individual items. And on any given item there may be a significant difference between its estimated cost and its actual cost. Inflationary increases can be estimated, but how can one estimate the costs of delays caused by sickness, union disputes, equipment breakdown, cancellations etc—in short, the cost of the unforeseen? Furthermore, an organization's detailed costs (both estimated and actual) must include similar costs submitted by all contractors and subcontractors.

In applying cost-benefit analysis to public relations, therefore, it must be emphasized that both costs and benefits may be either quantitative or qualitative, and neither costs nor benefits can always be precisely predicted.

In a Project Document, costs are always itemized and listed in a special section. Benefits, however, are not similarly listed. They appear in several sections of the document. All of the objectives, both final and intermediate, are considered benefits and additional ones are sometimes included among the justifications for objectives. There is no reason why all benefits could not be grouped into a second and special listing in the same section as the itemized costs. It would facilitate comparisons.

5. Evaluation

The Purposes of Evaluation

It is sometimes said that in evaluating a project one determines the extent to which it achieved its objectives. There is more to it than that. Some go further and add that in evaluation one also assesses the efficiency with which the project team operated. That too is important but there is still more.

The evaluation of a project is itself a project. It has its own objectives and its own methods for achieving them. The objectives of evaluation depend first of all on whether the organization is a steady-state system or self-steering (as described in Chapter 2). The primary objective of a steady-state system is its own stability; everything else is secondary (but not necessarily unimportant). Consider, for example, a small ethnic community trying to preserve its identity in a large city with a single dominant culture. The small community might stage a number of cultural events partly to make itself known and appreciated by the rest of the city's population but mainly to preserve its own culture by expressing it. If a cultural event was admired by others but resulted in some loss of interest among the young members of the ethnic minority (who might dislike traditional folk dances), the project would have failed even though the relationship between the minority group and the larger population might have been improved. Improved public relationships is not the community's primary objective. If it is a sufficiently important secondary one its cultural events might also be evaluated as public relations activities, but success or failure will ultimately be linked to the primary objective.

Evaluation in self-steering organizations

Public relations is of more direct concern to self-steering organizations, and project evaluation then becomes a more complex task. Self-steering organizations are those whose main objectives are outside of themselves. In pursuing their goals they set their course in response to any positive or negative feedback they receive. If their goals change, they change direction accordingly. If the goals remain fixed but circumstances change, they adjust to whatever demands that places on their steering capacity. Ideally they also monitor any internal changes which result from adjustments in their external course. All this information (regarding goal, external circumstances and internal functioning) these organizations then compare to their experience by recalling information from their memories. A self-steering organization therefore needs, as we have seen, reliable access to three kinds of information: information about its own past, information about its present structure and functioning, and information about its environment — that is, about its goal (whether fixed or changing) and the circumstances in which it must be pursued. For information about its own past the organization can access a data storage system, but it must systematically track down information about its present structure and operation and about its external world. The two principal means by which it does this are situation analysis and project evaluation. Situation analysis was discussed in Chapter 2; our concern now is with project evaluation, and we will discuss it as it applies to self-steering organizations (the less complex requirements of steady-state systems being included).

Think again of the example used in Chapter 2 — the car driver heading towards the kerb. He quickly estimates how far he is from the kerb and how fast he is going, then he changes course enough to avoid the kerb but not so much as to steer himself towards the opposite one. All of this transpires within seconds but during that short time the driver has received and processed the three types of information needed by a self-steering organization: information from his past experience as a driver, information about his external circumstances, and information about his own (and the car's) present condition and functioning. In this example every action the driver performs to stay on course can be considered as a tiny project. Each action has its own objectives and its own means for pursuing them. In order to adjust the course of the car he moves his arm to turn the steering wheel. But the arm-turning operation is a response to multiple inputs of sensory information, and the result of the arm-turning operation will not be simply the redirection of the car; there will be several results — the car's change of course, yes, but also a change in the driver's visual field, his emotional state, the car's speed, its stability and possibly its condition (a sudden jerk of the steering wheel could damage something). The driver's tiny project of turning his arm is thus the outcome of many causal influences and has many consequences. A proper evaluation of the arm-turning project would consider the degree to which it was adapted to the multiple needs that prompted it, the efficiency with which it was executed, and its various consequences.

Formative evaluation

An evaluation limited to determining whether a project fully attained its objectives ignores all other factors and possible effects. It is also a type of evaluation that can be carried out only after the project is finished. Equally necessary is a type carried out during the project to assure that its objectives and activities are always well adapted to the multiple needs that prompted it and to the circumstances in which it is implemented. Both needs and circumstances might, after all, change during the project's implementation. In the literature on evaluative research the evaluation done at the end of a project is called Summative Evaluation, that carried out during the project is called Formative Evaluation; both are necessary. Each must be based on the three types of information we have referred to: that drawn from the organization's experience; that relating to its present structure and functioning; and that concerning its goal and the external circumstances affecting the organization's pursuit of it.

Formative evaluation is a project within a project. It is an element of the main project and as such it commences and ends with it; but it has its own special objectives, different from (but complementing) those of the project. The objectives of formative evaluation are:

(1) To continually observe the direction and progress of the main project;
(2) To monitor its continuing effects on both its environment and the organization itself;
(3) To use all this information as a basis for deciding on either corrective or continuing action.

Formative evaluation is an assigned task, not a secondary chore attached to each team member's list of duties. The means for carrying it out are specified in the project plan and all necessary resources are allocated to it.

In pursuing their objectives, those responsible for formative evaluation seek to answer questions such as:

— Have the problems or opportunities that inspired the project changed since its conception?

— Have the circumstances in which the problem or opportunity exists changed significantly?
— Are resources adequate and are they being spent at the anticipated rate?
— What effects are the project's activities having within the organization?
— What effects are they having on the organization's environment—its physical environment, its business environment, the community in which it is located?
— Can any lessons be drawn from the organization's experience to guide the project's implementation?

Summative evaluation

Summative evaluation is a project which follows the completion of the main project but is inseparable from it. Like formative evaluation it has its own objectives and is allocated its own resources, but its main purpose is different from that of formative evaluation. It is important to a self-steering organization that information derived from its present operations be fed into its memory. Its reservoir of experience serves as a guide in future activities and as a benchmark for measuring progress. Summative evaluation provides some of the most important inputs to the organization's memory. Evaluators are of course concerned with the extent to which a project's objectives were attained, but their interests go beyond that. In a retrospective way they ask themselves all the questions which guided formative evaluation. For example, even if the project team worked efficiently, did the organization's continuing public relations programme suffer from having resources withdrawn from it to be used on the special project? Did the project engender negative side-effects which might in the long run offset the attainment of its main objectives? For example, a gay rights demonstration might have succeeded in bringing the social problems of homosexuals to public attention (its main objective) but did it also harden the attitudes of those opposed to the movement? What effects did the project have on the organization's structure? It can happen that certain departmental employees on being assigned to a project team were given increased responsibilities and authority. If they have worked well through the project they may be reluctant to return to their former positions when it is over.

It is worth mentioning too that summative evaluation, since it follows completion of a project, does not apply to continuing programmes; those programmes are continually assessed by formative evaluation.

In principle: *Summative evaluation is designed to draw from a particular project all the kinds of information needed by an organization to maintain its self-steering capacity* (or, in the case of a steady-state organization, to maintain its equilibrium). *Formative evaluation provides, in a continuous way, all the kinds of information needed by an organization in both projects and continuing programmes.*

What Evaluation Entails

To evaluate something is to pass a value judgement on it, to decide whether it is good or bad. In public relations it is to decide whether a project was a success, a partial success or a failure. That decision can obviously be made only after all the relevant facts have been gathered and analysed. Evaluation therefore entails research—the systematic gathering and analysis of information. An evaluator goes about his job with the same scientific discipline as the professional engaged in pre-planning research, and he employs many of the same methods.

Like the researcher doing situation analysis, the evaluator is interested in two types of information—quantitative and qualitative. Of the two, only quantitative information can be assembled and studied. Qualitative information, for example people's attitudes, can only be inferred from quantitative indicators. You cannot gather attitudes themselves for direct study, you can examine only the sensible manifestations of attitudes—responses to questionnaires, taped interviews, films etc. In most projects a variety of channels are used both for out-going and for in-coming information. Evaluation therefore nearly always includes the collation of such things as press cuttings, broadcast scripts, printed information materials, audit reports, speech texts, correspondence, accounting records, survey findings, audio-visual materials—in short, anything that can be physically examined. This collection includes not only materials used in planning or implementing the project itself, but also materials specially prepared for the evaluation. It may be necessary, for example, to carry out an opinion survey after the project to compare achievement to objectives. Also, unforeseen effects of a project cannot always be evaluated in the same pre-planned way as those which were targeted and for which resources were allocated. Because they were not foreseen, it is likely that no provision will have been made for their particular study. Evaluators will therefore have to design a suitable appraisal method and gather whatever information they need to apply it. Conceivably therefore, evaluation could call for special competencies and, as in pre-planning research, the question arises: who should do it? Since it is a type of scientific research, the same principle applies here as in situation analysis: *scientific, evaluative research is carried out only by people properly trained to do it.*

It does not follow that all evaluation must be assigned to specialists. If in planning a project a methodology for its evaluation was designed by a specialist, then it might be carried out by regular project team members; the evaluation design frequently calls for more scientific competence than its implementation. If, however, certain unforeseen project effects cannot be evaluated by the pre-planned method, then the project directors may have to call in a specialist. The author, for example, was once engaged in a project to attract voluntary workers to a health education programme in a particular region. The programme was so successful that observers from other regions later came to study it. This unexpected recognition inclined the original volunteers to pressure for salaries which, if acceded to, would have rendered the programme too costly to be continued. Nothing had been built into the programme evaluation design to accommodate this unforeseen effect. It therefore had to be studied separately by specialists.

Evaluative standards

Both formative and summative evaluation are related to decision making. Evaluators gather and analyse information in order to decide whether a project achieved its objectives, whether it was efficiently carried out, whether its overall benefits were worth the costs, whether team members performed competently, etc. But applying information to decision making requires that there are standards. The outcome of information analysis is compared to the standards and depending on how they correspond, one decides for or against. The word 'standards', notice, is in the plural. Evaluation is directed to many things and for each of them a separate standard is needed. Evaluators need, for example, efficiency standards to decide whether any time, effort, money or materials were wasted in achieving the project's results. They need performance standards to evaluate the work of team members, economy standards, quality standards, management standards, standards of discipline and morale. Not all of these standards are quantitative. For example, by what standards can one accurately evaluate the quality of an information pamphlet? The writing, the photographs, the artwork, layout and printing must all be judged by separate standards, and none of them is purely quantitative. Nor are there quantitative standards for assessing team spirit and discipline. It is impossible to contrive quantitative standards for measuring everything. Yet evaluators need firm standards, otherwise judgements become arbitrary and changeable and all control is lost. In practice, therefore, the important thing is that project team members know what their managers expect of them. Without always being able to put a precise figure on it, they must know what will be accepted, tolerated, rejected, praised, etc. These criteria, then, become the standards used in evaluation.

Why is Evaluation Neglected?

It frequently happens that public relations projects or continuing programmes are only casually evaluated; sometimes they are not evaluated at all. Since the case for rigorous scientific evaluation can be logically justified, one searches for equally strong arguments to explain the minor importance often assigned to it. The explanations are not logical, they are pragmatic.

Planning a project calls for as much detailed and time-consuming research as does evaluation, yet it is rarely skipped; why the difference? First of all, the consequences of neglect are more ominous in the planning stage than in the evaluation stage. A poorly planned project may well go wrong with effects that will be quickly and obviously disastrous. The consequences of neglecting evaluation, on the other hand, may not become apparent for years. The most serious effect will be the reduction in the organization's self-steering capacity. It will have deprived its memory of information needed to guide it into the future. But this is an intangible disadvantage immediately after a project's completion. Indeed, incumbent administrators may never have to deal with it; it may be a problem for the next generation. Of course no administrator would admit to having such a short-sighted view. More likely the neglect of project evaluation will be explained by a shortage of resources. By the end of the project the money may have run out, materials may be in short supply, and technical assistance contracts may have expired. But that does not imply that inadequate resources were allocated to the project, it more often reflects questionable priorities in deploying them. The fact that, at the end of the project, too few resources remained for evaluation means that the project administrators did not consider it important enough to merit an untouchable budget; so they dipped into it. Completing the project on time with here-and-now impressive results seemed more important than respecting the resources put aside for evaluation.

Belittling the importance of evaluation comes too, from a naive belief that it can be done without making an expensive fuss over it. If the project's main objectives are quantitative and readily observable, their attainment or non-attainment might very well be determined without much effort. But, as already pointed out, evaluation is concerned with much more than the attainment of project objectives. Most of what has to be evaluated is not quantitative and can be got at only through careful scientific effort.

Finally, and this may be most pertinent, evaluation may reveal that certain team members (possibly even project directors) performed incompetently. In determining the extent to which project objectives were achieved, evaluators also attempt to explain the degree to which they were not achieved. And if the non-achievement is explained by neglect or incompetence, this will be made known. Human nature and vested interests being what they are, pressure is sometimes exerted to avoid this.

The principle should be universal, but is not: *the importance of public relations project and programme evaluation is absolute.*

6. Specialized Public Relations

Why Specialization?

Public relations of any sort is always concerned with establishing and maintaining good relationships between organizations and their publics. To some degree this fundamental purpose argues against the need for any specialization within the profession. And indeed, not uncommonly practitioners cross from one field of practice to another with little difficulty. Nevertheless, specialization in public relations is on the increase. The explanation is rooted in social evolution.

Organizations, their publics and the circumstances in which they communicate with each other all change. Subtle changes may be accommodated routinely but sometimes the changes are profound, complicated and enduring. It can get to the point, and often does, where the special knowledge and skills needed to operate between an organization and its publics require that the practitioner gives to them his full attention. For example, increased life expectancy and declining birth rates have combined to age our population. At the same time, increased unemployment has forced many people into compulsory retirement. As a consequence the 'public' of unemployed and relatively poor old people has become a new and important one to many organizations. To some degree the problems of this new public are those of all other unemployed people, but these people are also old which makes a difference; their poverty creates problems similar to those faced by all poor people, but it is complicated by the fact that they are old and generally unemployable; and while their age identifies them with all other aging people, their poverty and forced unemployment make them different.

To complicate matters further, the members of this new public live in an environment very different from that in which they spent most of their lives. Technology has altered styles and standards of living; social ethics have changed for example, with respect to human reproduction; social relationships have changed, for example regarding cohabitation and child raising; systems of communication, transport and medical care have changed, as have forms of religious practice. The psychological effects of all this on old people can be serious. A public relations practitioner representing a social agency working with them might find that his work calls for special research and the development of unique skills. And there are any number of such new publics today: drug addicts, computer fanatics, all the protest groups—against racism, sexism, nuclear energy, heterosexualism, etc—and groups fighting for political, religious, cultural or linguistic independence. All of these special-interest publics have special needs and demands; they therefore exert special pressures on the organizations with which they have to deal. The result, in the field of public relations, is twofold: (a) many organizations find that they must adapt their structure, policies and functions to meet the new demands (and this adaptation may be continual); (b) they must be represented by practitioners who fully comprehend these organizational changes and at the same time understand the new publics and have the skills to work with them. Not surprisingly, various special forms of public relations practice have emerged.

In chapter 3 we discussed the practitioner's problem of trying to arrange between his organization and its publics an exchange of self-portraits. Since he is the principal agent in this exchange, it requires that he first get to know both of them as fully as possible. This fundamental requirement does not change in the case of the specialist. The difference is that he limits his professional concern to either a particular type of organization or a particular category of publics. It is a matter of effectiveness: the special nature of certain public relationships is such that the practitioner must give his full time and attention to them. They are complicated to start with and they constantly evolve. Frequently too, there is little or no experience from which one can learn. The conditions that create the new demands are often unprecedented.

Determinants of specialization

Any form of public relations practice could become a specialization. A public relations firm might choose to limit its practice in this way, as might an individual practitioner, or a consultancy might list certain types of practice as specialized. In any case the decision is not arbitrary, it is principled—the principle being: *The requirements of the relationships between certain types of organization and certain publics determine the need for specialization.* It is therefore impossible to draw up a comprehensive list of specializations. The following are mentioned by way of example: governmental (at all levels), medical, international, financial, educational, religious, industrial, political and public relations for voluntary organizations. In each case the expertise required of the practitioner is considerable. Take, for example, financial public relations. A practitioner, in addition to his basic knowledge and skills, might be required to understand company law, banking and finance, the stock exchange, bid procedures, the operation of various government commissions, boardroom practice, the nature and operations of financial institutions, and the policies and operation of financial communications media. One does not develop such expertise casually. Specialization may require formal study, more often the newcomer to a firm is given a thorough briefing then serves what amounts to an apprenticeship. The danger in this approach is that it often perpetuates established ways of doing things. The apprentice feels it is not for him to suggest changes until he has become a full-fledged team member; but by that time he is so familiar with the team's operational style he may not care to change it—especially if he has been commended for the way he 'fits into' the organization. Recently graduated students who included public relations in their study programmes are sometimes held in check by employees who never studied it. It is felt that the fledgling must learn how things run in the 'real world' before his opinions are to be fully respected.

In the rest of this chapter we will take a look at three examples of specialized public relations. In each case the emphasis is on points generally overlooked rather than complete coverage. They are offered here to suggest the thoroughness which the specialized practitioner brings to his job; no detail is unimportant. The author chose these three examples after reading the cursory treatment given them in some available public relations textbooks.

Public Relations for Voluntary Organizations

A voluntary organization (VO) differs from a commercial organization in that the VO does not sell products or services. Many do provide valuable services, but frequently the VO's primary concern is the promotion of values. These may be either values in their own right (for example, democracy) or values which legitimize a cause (for example, justice as a motive for opposing racism). Of the two, the second is the more common and tactically difficult.

The successful promotion of a cause depends first on whether the values underlying it fit into the value system of the public being approached, and secondly on whether the public is favourably disposed towards the promoting organization. Winning public acceptance both of the cause and of itself is the fundamental public relations task of VOs. The relationships involved can therefore be thought of as forming a triangle, the three terminals being the VO, the public and the cause. However, there are not just three but four resulting orientations: VO to public, public to VO, VO to cause, and public to cause.

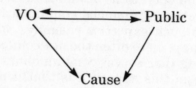

A healthy two-way relationship between the VO and any of its publics is most likely to survive if their individual attitudes towards the cause are the same, for example if they both oppose vivisection or support cancer research. If they differ in their attitudes towards the cause their relationship to each other will suffer stress. It might, though, be strong enough to survive. For example, at the time of this writing Britain is in disagreement with the other members of the Commonwealth on the use of economic sanctions to exert pressure on the government of South Africa to eliminate apartheid. However, their alliance seems strong enough to survive this disagreement. In a situation where the alliance between a VO and one of its publics is tenuous and they disagree on the merits of a cause, the result can be disastrous: the public might separate itself from the organization. To avoid this the organization must strengthen its relationship with the public in order to gain time to redesign its appeal, basing it on values more deeply respected by the public.

The nature of the cause

The case of a public relations consultancy which has contracted to promote a cause is different. Not itself being committed to the cause, it may have the option of terminating the contract, an option which may be advisable. If it encounters powerful and widespread opposition to its promotional efforts, the consultancy might prefer to dissociate itself from the cause in order to preserve its own public respect.

At the moment, however, we are concerned only with VOs which either cannot abandon their cause without disbanding (for example, 'Friends of the Trepassy Philharmonic Orchestra') or choose not to do so. Such organizations must always concern themselves with all four of the orientations mentioned above. Of the four, an alliance between the organization and its publics is the most important. If that relationship is strong and positive in both directions, usually the VO and its publics will be in accord on the cause. But even if they disagree, they might (as already mentioned) be able to negotiate an agreement on the basis of their alliance.

Collaborative public relations

The situation becomes considerably more complicated when a VO collaborates with a commercial organization to promote a cause. For example, an organization for the protection of animals might join forces with a pet food company. Success in such cases depends on the two-way relationships between each organization and its publics, between each organization and the other one's publics, and between the VO and the pet food company. Then there are several important one-way relationships: that of the VO to the cause, that of the pet food company to the cause, that of their combined publics to the cause, and finally the attitude of the VO's publics to the product, in this case the pet food. If the pet food is not popular with the VO's publics, the organization might suffer from associating itself with the manufacturer. Similarly, the cause will suffer if for any reason either the VO or the pet food company loses public acceptance. The advantages of a collaboration between a VO and a commercial organization can be considerable but the risks must be carefully considered and strategies well planned.

Appropriate values

Another point: in public relations related to a cause, it is important that the values appealed to be those honestly considered appropriate by the VO. (Of course one hopes they will also be respected by its publics and by those who are to benefit from the cause.) This does not go without saying. It sometimes happens that inappropriate values are used simply because they work more reliably. Consider, for example, a campaign for famine relief in Africa. The campaign poster might (as is often the case) feature a photograph of an emaciated black child, hand extended, begging for help. Both the photo and the message reflect the hope that people will be moved by pity to respond with charity. A more honest appeal would be based on justice. The people who consume most of the world's food supply are being asked to help those who are starving. Given every man's right to an appropriate share of the world's resources, we insult starving people when we portray them as beggars appealing to our charity, as if they had no strict right to what they ask for. The right to life implies the right to eat. Nevertheless, inappropriate appeals to charity still abound. Why? Because they work better, or so it is thought.

If the VO honestly thinks that charity is the appropriate value it could be discredited for its lack of logic. If it realizes that famine relief is a matter of justice but appeals to charity in the hope of raising more money, it risks having its hypocrisy recognized. Why then do such questionable appeals generally work? Because people hesitate to even suspect that a voluntary organization speaking on behalf of starving people could be either hypocritical or intellectually feeble. Communications from VOs invariably touch our moral sensibilities and we expect honourable moral standards of people who approach us in that way; too, unless the message is purely saccharine we expect its intellectual content to be well reasoned. If the underpinnings of these two assumptions crumble, the whole structure will collapse. People have been known to 'swear off' certain VOs for such reasons—and understandably. On the other hand, some VOs have improved their performance after re-examining the slant of their appeals.

Language

Finally, there is a delicate question of language in public relations for VOs. To best assure that a message is effective, it should be expressed in the vernacular of those for whom it is intended. The recipient of a message is best approached on the language level of his own social class not because he might otherwise be put off but because he might otherwise ignore the message. Imagine a tramp's reaction to the offer of a free subscription to *The Economist*. He would not likely be offended by the offer but might well refuse it with a casual shrug. He simply could not care less— even if he knew that much of the magazine's subject matter might interest him. *The Economist* does not address itself to his social class, and that is clearly evidenced in its language.

Why is this of special concern to public relations officers for VOs? It very often happens that VOs address themselves to people of affluence; after all, they are generally soliciting donations. But if you speak to the affluent in their middle- or upper-class language there is a slight danger that you may be suspected of sharing their affluence, in which case the appeal would lose some of its power. In other words, if you speak to them in their own language you risk alienating them; but if you fail to meet them on their own level you risk being ignored—as the tramp ignores *The Economist*. It is a delicate situation which calls for sensibility to the nuance of language, and a solid unquestionable honesty. It is not a time to be glib.

Public Relations for Religious Organizations

Suppose a religious organization opts for professional management of its public relations. At what level of executive authority should the public relations officer function? There can be no pat answer: the situation is extremely complicated. Three main elements have to be aligned: the structure of the religious organization, the nature of public relations concerns, and the general structure of commercial and public service organizations.

Organizational structure

Consider the religious organization first. It may be an international organization, a national one, a regional assembly or perhaps a single local congregation. An international religious organization is generally governed by a legislative body of some kind, with a single person perhaps exercising privileged authority within it. In each country in which the religious community exists, there may be a national governing body to which several regional governors are responsible. However, this is not always so. Sometimes each regional authority answers directly to the international governing body. In any case, subject to the regional governors there are generally several lower levels of jurisdiction eventually reaching the congregations of believers. These lowest-level communities are usually served by a very small number of clergy (frequently just one) who conduct their business in a house and provide religious services in a place specifically set aside for that purpose.

At each level of jurisdiction (international, national, regional and/or local) there generally exists not only a recognized governing authority, but also a number of administrative or consultative bodies in the service of that authority. These are usually called boards, commissions, councils, offices etc and each is responsible for certain matters of special interest to the religious organization. Some are concerned solely with purely administrative matters, for example the organization's finances, property holdings or buildings; others deal with moral questions, doctrinal matters, social problems etc. As might be expected, their jurisdictions often overlap.

The nature of concern

Consider now the matters of concern to a public relations department. These include all problems or opportunities which might affect the quality of the organization's rapport with various publics. Clearly no natural limits can be put on these concerns. They could be ecumenical matters, questions of education, racial tensions, matters of social justice, public health, national security, almost anything in fact. As well, they might be international problems or they could affect only a limited jurisdiction—national, regional or local. It seems then, there is no unique location for a public relations department within the structure of a major religious organization. The scope of public relations will invariably overlap the domains of several other departments at various levels of administrative authority. However, this is not an impasse.

Public relations problems are not essentially distinct from all others; rather, most problems of concern to a religious organization have a public relations dimension as well as their own special character. If the organization becomes involved in a problem of racial discrimination, for example, it could be that the only solution would be a local government policy change. The central problem might therefore best be handled between the local authority and an appropriate religious committee. But the repercussions of the problem might affect several publics—all racial minorities in the community, local employers, social service agencies etc. These extended effects would be public relations problems. Furthermore, attitudes engendered by a social problem can endure long after the problem itself has been solved at the policy level. It is these attitudes, more than anything else, that affect public relations. They might even harden into convictions that could motivate discriminatory behaviour for years.

Conceivably, therefore, a public relations office could be established within a religious organization at any jurisdictional level or, for that matter, at every level. At times it might operate independently of other offices, at other times it might collaborate with them. The public relations office would of course have no authority to resolve questions of dogma, morals, liturgy, church law, etc but it would have the expertise to detect and handle the effects of those problems on public dispositions. At the same time, a permanently established public relations office would conduct continuing situation analysis within its territory of responsibility. The benefit of this would be that future problems and opportunities might be foreseen—not just public relations problems, but a variety of problems many of which would directly concern specialized offices within the organization.

Levels of jurisdiction

Although a public relations office, as we just said, could *conceivably* be established at any jurisdictional level, in practice some levels are better than others. Carrying out a public relations project or a continuing programme frequently requires that decisions are made promptly. If the public relations officer is far removed from the organization's decision makers his practice will lose its vitality. However, if the highest level of management is too distant from regional or local authorities, it may be best for the public relations officer to answer directly to an intermediate level of management. For example, an international religious organization will have its headquarters in a particular location. Normally the governing body at headquarters will exercise authority over national governing bodies in different parts of the world, and local and regional authorities will respond to national authority. If the public relations officer is directly responsible to the highest authority he might be unable to respond quickly to demands at the national or regional levels. As well, the cultural context of national problems might require that they be resolved by people of that culture rather than by culturally different people recommended only by their professional competence.

Ideally the director of public relations should participate in the decision-making authority which implements policy and allocates resources throughout the geographic area of his responsibility. If, for example, he is responsible for public relations in an ecclesiastical province he should share provincial management authority. But this principle can be pushed too far. We have just mentioned some problems of a practitioner having too much authority; consider now a public relations officer having too little — one working at the parish level, for example. According to the principle just stated, he would have no more administrative authority than the pastor or priest. But this would probably be inadequate. The factors which influence public dispositions seldom operate exclusively within the territorial limits of a parish. Prejudice does not stop at parish boundaries, nor do rumours, mass communications or the influence of various activist groups. The area of responsibility assigned to a public relations officer should therefore not be too small. There is a cut-off point below which he cannot operate effectively. There are no rules for identifying that point, but one might be guided by the broadcast range of local radio and television stations. After all, the extent of the public relations officer's influence is very much determined by the range of the communications media he uses. Obviously broadcast areas will not correspond to ecclesiastical territories but they could provide a basis for negotiating the jurisdiction of the public relations officer. But this is only a suggestion: the important point is that he must have whatever authority he needs to do his job effectively. Too much might separate him from people at the field level; too little will enfeeble him.

Levels of authority

There is a third problem in situating the public relations function in a religious organization's structure. The public relations officer not only represents the organization in dealing with certain publics, to some degree he also speaks for those publics to his employer. It therefore falls to the public relations officer to get to know the publics in order to make their dispositions known to the religious organization. However, some of these publics exercise civic authority, some are professional groups, some may be rather high-level figures in other religious communities. To deal effectively with such people the public relations officer may be required to hold a fairly high level of authority in his own organization. There is perhaps an element of snobbishness in this but it is nevertheless true that most executives prefer to do business with people at their own level. And they frequently measure stature in terms of decision-making authority. If the public relations officer is perceived as a low-level functionary, he may not be able to work well with people who are clearly above him in executive authority. Again, there is no simple rule for settling the matter; it calls for political acumen.

Properly locating the office of public relations is not the only problem faced by a religious organization that chooses to go in that direction. Other problems relate, for example, to the selection of a public relations director. Must he accept the belief system of the organization? Should he be a cleric or a layman? Does he need special theological training? These practical considerations go beyond the scope of this book. But underlying them is an important principle: in religious organizations, public relations as a management function must be distinguished from public relations as evangelism. (This book deals solely with public relations as a management function.) The necessary qualifications for the performance of each function may differ. And the final judgement as to what they are and who possesses them remains with the directorship of the organization. Some guidance with respect to the professional qualifications of a public relations director is offered in the final chapter of this book.

A case study

The relationships which any religious organization has with its publics are primarily determined by religious beliefs and traditional practices. Since these beliefs and practices are fundamental to the very existence of his client organization, the public relations practitioner accepts them as given, never to be manipulated or overlooked and to be questioned only with genuine respect. Ironically, this can cause complications. Consider, for example, a particular (and true) case, that of a community of Roman Catholic missionary priests which we will call simply 'The Society'. The members of The Society (approximately 200) were all priests, most of whom worked in other countries — 'on the missions' as they said. These were either non-Christian countries where the priests' task was to establish the Catholic Church, or Latin American countries where there were too few native priests to serve the number of Catholic people.

The Society's public relations department, accommodated in its headquarters, had three stated objectives:

(1) To encourage young Catholic men to join The Society;
(2) To raise money to finance The Society's operation;
(3) To encourage Catholic people to support The Society's work with their prayers.

In pursuit of these objectives The Society published a monthly magazine, conducted three direct-mail fund-raising appeals each year, and as often as possible sent priests to speak in parish churches, Catholic schools and to various organizations across the country. Three priests, one public relations officer and an administrative staff of eight lay people were permanently assigned to the department and at times as many as four additional priests were appointed to help out temporarily.

Depending heavily as it did on its monthly magazine and direct-mail appeals, The Society made every effort to maintain an active and ever-growing mailing list. New names were received from churches where collections for The Society were taken up. Donations were made in envelopes distributed for that purpose, each designed to record the name and address of the donor. These people thereafter received the magazine and annual appeals. The mailing list was subdivided by geographical region and by the amount of money that people contributed annually. Thus one could readily identify large, average and modest donors from each region of the country and from each city, town and village within each region. These groups, as well as male Catholic students and a few voluntary organizations established to support

The Society, were the publics of direct concern to the public relations department. The Superior General of The Society and his advisory Council dealt directly with several other key publics, notably the bishops and priests in the home country upon whose co-operation they depended for access to Catholic people.

Influence of belief

We come now to the influence of Catholic religious belief on The Society's public relations programme. Although The Society's publics were clearly defined, no attempt was ever made by the public relations department to get to know them; no study was ever carried out to determine their precise attitudes towards missionary work and The Society. (The bishops of the home country were the single exception. Their attitudes towards The Society were crucially important and The Society's Superior General always kept himself and his Council aware of them.) All publics other than the bishops were in a sense lumped into one: they were all Roman Catholics bound by an obligation inherent in their faith to help spread the Church throughout the world. That was all The Society felt it had to know about them. Any other information might have been interesting but, at the end of the day, was not essential. The Society's benefactors were also assumed to understand that the priests who appealed to them for support were representatives of Christ. These two parameters defined the mutual understanding The Society considered essential to its public relations function. They were not by any means naive premises; they were as solid as the Catholic faith which the priests and people shared. But they paled at any suggestion that public attitudes should be further explored. To base an appeal for support on anything other than the faith would be to secularize it, to demonstrate a lack of trust in God's providence. Human motivations were appealed to only in the context of the faith. For example, reference was made to the poverty of God's people in most mission countries, to the spiritual deficiency of non-Christian lives, to the self-sacrifice of priests who had left their homes and country to perpetuate the work of Christ's apostles. But purely human motivations, for example the possibility of social or cultural enrichment of other peoples through the work of the priests, never featured in The Society's appeals.

One might have thought that apart from the appeals—for funds, prayers and recruits—The Society would have engaged in a continuing programme directed towards mutual understanding between itself and its publics. It went a little in this direction: it tried, principally through its monthly magazine, to reveal itself somewhat to its publics. But again, no attempt was ever made to get to know them. They were Catholic people, members of Christ's 'Mystical Body', and that was all that had to be known.

This is a good example of the influence of Management mentality on public relations programming (discussed in Chapter 3). It can happen that objectives and the means for pursuing them are determined not only by logic and feasibility but also by Management dispositions. In this case, the belief system set limits that overruled pragmatism.

Traditional practice

The Society's public relations officer was of two minds about all this. On the one hand he appreciated the solidity of the base on which The Society built its relationships with its publics, but on the other hand he could not help feeling that the relationships would be enriched through greater mutual understanding. However, in trying to make this case with The Society's directors, he encountered the second policy kingpin—traditional practice.

The Roman Catholic Church is hierarchical, every member being precisely located in the chain of command that extends from the Pope to the newly baptized infant. The clergy, of course, are most aware of this. A 'vagrant' cleric is forbidden by canon law. A priest is ordained as the subject of either a bishop or the superior of a community of priests, and he cannot be freed from that authority before being accepted as the subject of another bishop or superior. In the case of The Society it was the Superior General who with his advisory Council exercised authority over all member priests, he himself being subject to the Vatican. The public relations officer was responsible to the priest-director of the public relations department who, in turn, answered to the Superior General. The lines of communication were always vertical and messages which flowed downward invariably had their origins in secret meetings. The public relations officer and the director of his department were occasionally summoned to meetings of the Council but only to explain matters related to their work. They were never allowed to attend meetings at which decisions were made.

The members of The Society did not resent the secrecy of Council meetings. They recognized it as conforming fully with the traditions of the Catholic Church. Furthermore, it was a matter of faith with them that the deliberations of their superiors were guided by the Holy Spirit. While they might disagree with Council decisions, they never questioned their providential nature; and the public relations officer was expected not to question it either, even when decisions went against what he considered preferable policy. Conversely, the Superior General and his Council believed that the same Divine providence was evident in the behaviour of The Society's members. While a paternal authority was exercised to maintain order, it was again a matter of faith that the behaviour of individual priests could never seriously threaten The Society's status as an instrument in God's redemptive plan for the world. And the public relations officer was viewed in the same way: he was an element in a providential plan. If he contributed to The Society's work, God would be thanked; if he failed, his failure would be accepted with resignation to God's permissive will. His personal problem was to maintain any sense of urgency under those conditions.

His was a practice different from that of most in the public relations profession. While other practitioners sometimes complained of being excluded from their boards of directors, The Society's public relations officer experienced the full declension of that separation: the Superior General and his Council, from which the officer was isolated, were themselves infinitely distanced from the mysterious deliberations of the Holy Trinity who ultimately guided their destiny. The officer's occasional sense of powerlessness was, however, assuaged by a sense of freedom: he was assured that either success or failure had from eternity been positioned in a Divine plan of redemption. Not many practitioners work with that assurance.

Public Relations for Arts Organizations

Public relations practitioners working for arts organizations are sometimes warned that artists are hypersensitive and must be treated carefully (as though promotion of the arts would be simpler if the artist could be eliminated). If difficulties exist between artists and public relations practitioners, they should not unthinkingly be put down to the artist's mythical hypersensitivity. They are more likely explained by the fact that the antagonists are engaged in opposite types of work and too often neither makes a serious effort to understand what the other is up to. Perhaps they should share the task of getting to know each other, but since the practitioner and not the artist has chosen the pursuit of mutual understanding as a career, the initiative more logically falls to him.

The practitioner who looks into this question may be stunned to discover that the artist, as an artist, is dedicated to uselessness. It is not that the things he produces are essentially useless — artists have produced magnificent and useful churches, railway stations, national anthems, tombs and even door knockers—but the artistic quality of these things is a useless extra. An ugly church can be every bit as useful as a beautiful one. Artistic quality is unnecessary to the function of a church or anything else. It is in that sense that Paul Valéry (1972, p.26) says, 'The most evident characteristic of a work of art may be termed uselessness.'

But to say that the work of art is useless is not to say that the artist has no purpose in creating it. He certainly does have a purpose. Etienne Gilson (1957, p.176) is very clear on this point. The immediate purpose of the artist, he says, is his own pleasure; he creates something that gives him a unique kind of pleasure, one that cannot be stimulated either by anything in nature or by any other work of art. It should be evident, by the way, that we are talking here about genuine artists not the mass producers of pretty pictures, catchy tunes and greeting card verses. A true artist works primarily for the aesthetic satisfaction he derives from his own creation, which explains why Vincent Van Gogh could live with wild enthusiasm in abject poverty producing paintings which, during his lifetime, very few people wanted to buy. Van Gogh could undoubtedly have lived more handsomely if people had paid him the prices his paintings command today; however, any reading of his life clearly reveals that he felt much more rewarded by those who appreciated his paintings than by the few who purchased them as decorations. Which brings us to the artist's second purpose—providing aesthetic satisfaction to others.

Art and pleasure

Paul Valéry (1973, p.27) having made the point that a work of art is essentially useless went on to say that, nevertheless, 'among our useless impressions there are some that may take hold of us and make us wish to prolong or renew them.' In other words, a work of art may stimulate pleasure in the observer—a special kind of pleasure, a kind that wants to be prolonged. A useful product satisfies a need in being used (having used the can opener you put it away), a work of art stimulates a desire for more of the pleasure it evokes. Not all works of art stimulate the same response in all observers, they may even leave some people cold. That doesn't matter: the observer's response is the artist's secondary purpose. Even if nobody else likes his work, if he himself finds it pleasurable he has succeeded.

Because they cannot find in the world around them objects that evoke the kind of pleasure they seek and want to bring to other people, artists create those things. They create a world that

125

would otherwise not exist. And the elements of that world, the works of art, may bear no resemblance whatsoever to the elements of our world. It is not required of a work of art that it resemble anything we have seen, heard or experienced before. It is a unique being, brought into existence to evoke a unique pleasure. And a world of such unique beings constitutes a unique world. Artists 'live in a universe of their own,' Gilson (1957, p.182) says, 'a sort of earthly paradise.'

Art in the world economy

But all is not well in paradise. Poverty and suicide may have been acceptable to Vincent Van Gogh but most artists prefer at least a touch of comfortable security. Some unashamedly long for the good life. They therefore want to make money from their work. As a consequence of that understandable sentiment, the production and consumption of works of art are no longer independent of each other. Art, even the finest, has taken its place in the world economy, a world of utilitarian values. Most artists, however, are not themselves capable of handling this side of their business. They therefore have agents or managers whose job it is to assure their clients' financial survival without disturbing their artistic privacy. A manager can be a marketing wizard without knowing much about the arts, the difference between the two is that real. It is a distinction that also explains state involvement in the administration of the arts. One has no particular reason to expect a politician or civil servant to be an artist, yet today the state has assumed responsibility for the establishment of arts councils to 'encourage' artists, the preservation of works of art, the propaganda uses of art, the management of lucrative art exhibitions, and the establishment in law of ownership rights. The art world now has its own media, its own schools and educational philosophies, its own markets and banks (museums, libraries etc), its own historical and cultural functions, even its own foreign and domestic policies. And an enormous agglomeration of people are employed in this administrative side of the arts—including a goodly number of public relations practitioners.

The practitioner and the artist

The main difference between artists and those who administer the arts is not that artists are the more sensitive; it is that the true artist still sees his work as essentially useless, while administrators (as such) are concerned with art only as something useful. The public relations practitioner perhaps has more reason than his fellow administrators to try to understand the artist and his world, but unless he himself is an artist by talent, training and temperament he has to accept the fact that he belongs to another world. And it is not his function to try, however diplomatically, to coax the artist from his privacy into the hustle and bustle of the 'real world'. The effective practitioner, on the contrary, preserves an absolute respect for the artist's perception of his unique work and world. He realizes that while a work of art may be put to some respectable uses it remains always a product intended primarily to give pleasure, first to the artist himself then possibly to others. The distinction between commercial art and what is called 'fine art' might be helpful here: commercial art is produced to be used, fine art is produced to be enjoyed; although useful commercial art is at times artistically beautiful and fine art can at times be put to good use, the two must never be confused. They are different. Similarly, the 'useless' artist can at times become a functionary (giving a lecture, conducting a workshop, attending an opening-night cocktail party) and the 'useful' public relations practitioner might muse periodically on the sequestered artistic world of uselessness. But again, the two should not be confused.

Evaluating arts public relations

Art appreciation defies quantitative analysis. But paradoxically, public relations for the arts can to some degree be measured in quantitative terms. Most products marketed for public consumption offer a combination of functional and design features. A person may buy a car primarily for its use but is seldom indifferent to its appearance. Even shiny red apples sell better than scruffy ones. Conversely works of art, although primarily aesthetic, frequently offer functional benefits. Attendance at a symphony concert may be a social function; a fine painting may add character to a room. But a car that won't work gains no points for being stylish, and a poor painting is discounted as a work of art even if it admirably covers a rough spot on a wall. At the end of the day, therefore, patrons of the arts support an *essentially* useless industry, yet their support can be largely measured in terms of funding, record purchases, attendance at performances and the like. The price that one pays for a sculpture is not a direct measurement of its beauty, but if its beauty was not appreciated the piece would likely not have been purchased. In other words, quantitative indicators (purchases, attendance etc.) reflect to some degree an appreciation of art's useless beauty, no matter what functional benefits may also be involved.

Therefore, while the public relations practitioner must respect the artists' commitment to beauty, he may rightfully be guided in his work by measurable indicators (albeit partial) of its public appreciation.

7. Training for Public Relations

The Unpredictable Future

In 1937 a team of American and French 'experts' ventured to predict the scientific and technological developments which would appear by 1955. They failed to foresee television, radar, antibiotics, atomic energy or the transistor. This anecdote is recounted by Michel Poniatowski, Director of the Commission on Energy, Research and Technology for the European Parliament, in his book *Les Technologies Nouvelles* (1986, p.28) as evidence of the impossibility of accurately forecasting the world's technological future. Poniatowski also mentions the Director of the US Patent Office who gave up his job in 1899 explaining, 'Why stay? There is nothing more to invent.'

Today, nobody believes that there is nothing more to invent but no one is rash enough to make confident predictions. Poniatowski himself goes about as far as one might dare. He groups the new technologies into four clusters: bio-technology, new materials, new forms of energy, and electronics (including informatics). There will, he says, be significant developments in each cluster but the rapidity of evolution will derive from combinations of clusters. For example, developments in electronics will be accelerated by the introduction of new materials, and bio-technology will benefit from what happens in the field of electronics. Among the more spectacular innovations already to emerge from the interaction of electronics and bio-technology is the Fifth Generation Computer developed in Japan. Poniatowski describes it this way: 'Il s'agit d'un "cerveau" semblable à celui de l'homme, et un jour peut-être, supérieur à celui d l'homme...' (Poniatowski, 1986, p.168). (It concerns a 'brain' comparable to that of man and one day perhaps superior to that of man.)

The effects of new technologies on patterns of employment is a major concern in all industrialized countries. It is a foregone conclusion that unemployment will rise sharply in certain sectors while new jobs will be created in others, but the precise distribution of these changes cannot be foreseen nor can their ramifications. Unquestionably the consequences for public relations will be serious. A company that once employed 1000 labourers but now achieves higher levels of production with 100 robots and 10 employees, has undergone a fundamental change. Any mutual understanding that once existed between itself and its publics (including the labour force and their dependents) must now be re-examined.

Public relations is not an industry with firmly established ways of doing things—at least it should not be. It manages relationships, and the only relationships that never change are between parties that never change. If the parties evolve, the relationship must evolve accordingly and those responsible for its maintenance must find new ways to manage it. It is therefore the essence of public relations to be flexible and innovative. The degree to which it feels threatened by social and technological change is a measure of the degree to which it has become attached to its operational style; and that, in turn, is a measure of the degree to which it has misunderstood its function.

New technologies are not a threat to public relations but they certainly pose a challenge. They will create new industries and drastically change many established ones. What's more, the rhythm of these changes will be rapid. A new industry may have a life expectancy of no more than 10 or 15 years before being rendered obsolete by still more advanced technologies. The only permanent organizations may be a relatively few giant international corporations masterminding the operations of an ever-changing corps of short-lived subsidiaries. And as often as the configuration of parent firms and subsidiaries changes, the composition of publics changes. What does mutual understanding between an organization and its publics mean in such circumstances? Can it possibly be achieved? This is the challenge to public relations.

New technologies will affect not only industrial structures, they will affect our way of life. When one compares today's industrialized cities to what they were 50 years ago, the differences are not merely technological. It is not just that we now have television, computers, jet travel, sophisticated medical centres and polyester clothes. Our vision of life has changed—our values, attitudes and beliefs; our social relationships and institutions have changed—marriage, education, class structures, political institutions. The relationships between technological change, social change and attitudinal change are extremely subtle. They act on each other; each is both cause and effect. Again, the challenge to public relations is not merely to help publics understand the impact of technological change, but to establish understanding in new social and attitudinal settings. New technologies may be fearfully resisted by many people; some even oppose them on moral grounds. Will their attitudes change in a few years? The public acceptance of companies using these new technologies might very well depend on public attitudes towards the integration of life and science. It is the business of public relations to counsel organizations on the best routes to public understanding: not an easy task.

The Need for Breadth and Depth

How, then, might one prepare for a career in public relations? The guideposts are breadth and depth. Public relations is not a profession for glib, shallow performers who have mastered a limited vocabulary of slick jargon; and it is not for people who feel accomplished. It is for solidly trained people who realize they will never outgrow the need for further education. It is for people who can adapt to the unexpected without losing their balance. A university degree in public relations may be helpful when one is searching for a first job, but it might misleadingly suggest that one has little more to learn. In any case, since few universities offer such degrees it seems more practical to consider the training a public relations practitioner needs to do his job well, with or without a university degree.

An education programme in public relations can be no more stable than the mix of knowledge and skills demanded by the profession, and the point has just been made that the mix continually changes. What are proposed here are basic courses. Their content and application would have to be adapted to changing circumstances, but collectively they would form a good foundation.

Basic training

Since public relations will always entail communicating with publics within the framework of their beliefs, attitudes, opinions and forms of behaviour, both theoretical and practical courses in sociology and mass communications are essential. One should understand the nature of society, social structure and function, social change, stability and interaction. Sociological skills should include research methods and statistical analysis. Theories of communication are important, as well as the sociology of mass communication, models of communication and control (cybernetics), semiotics and the process of persuasion. The essential communication skills are taught in journalism courses. They include basic writing and reporting, feature writing, editing and all forms of audio-visual production.

Given the close link between public relations and management, especially in commercial organizations, practitioners should understand the fundamentals of business administration—types of management, accounting, finance, advertising, labour relations, marketing, consumer affairs and perhaps shareholder relations.

Finally, some basic courses in psychology would be helpful, particularly group psychology and what is sometimes called 'mob' psychology, as well as models of leadership and of attitudinal and behavioural change.

If, before entering the profession, one has already decided to specialize in a particular type of public relations, certain other courses might also be required. For example, one could hardly enter governmental public relations without some knowledge of political science and the structure of national and local government. Similarly, public relations for a large international industry might call for an understanding of international trade and commerce and possibly some competence in a second language.

Continuing education

But basic training alone will no longer suffice. Given the pace of social change, the inevitability of new modes of production and new relationships between management and labour, the emergence of new product and service industries and a reordering of priorities among those already established, it is unthinkable that public relations practitioners will be able to turn their hand to the new situation without any further training. It will be a matter of professional and psychological survival. To find oneself floundering in a situation where the pace of change accelerates inexorably can be terrifying. The only realistic hope for the public relations practitioner lies in a continual updating of his qualifications.

Can public relations be taught?

To insist upon the importance of education to public relations practice does not mean that public relations can be learned as one might learn how to cook. Public relations is a search for mutual understanding between an organization and its publics. That is a notoriously elusive objective. Two people seldom achieve complete mutual understanding. Two negotiating teams stand a lesser chance. What chance does a national (or multinational) corporation have to attain a perfect meeting of minds and sentiments with its innumerable publics? None, I would say. And if the final objective is unattainable, it is a contradiction in terms to say that one can be taught how to achieve it.

Public relations survives as a profession only because practitioners set themselves limited objectives—modest enough to be realistic. These objectives fall short of complete mutual understanding but they include such things as: effective communication, a sensitive monitoring of public responses, reliable estimates of environmental trends, measurements of operational efficiency, and evaluation of programme results. All of these things, even if done magnificently, will not deliver mutual understanding; but mutual understanding cannot even be approached unless these limited tasks are performed well. And one can learn how to perform them well.

In addition, education can help one develop an intellectual sensitivity important to public relations. In studying the various subjects linked to public relations, one benefits as much from appreciating their unrealized potential as from a knowledge of what has been accomplished through them. For example, while it is helpful to know how institutions have contributed to the quality of social life, it is just as important to be able to project from those accomplishments to a vision of what might yet be attained through well-informed creativity. Education helps one to make such projections not by providing clear-cut routes into the future, but by encouraging individual initiative and honouring courageous imagination.

References

Deutsch, K. (1963) *The Nerves of Government* The Free Press of Glencoe, New York.

Eysenck, H. J. et al (eds) (1972) *The Encyclopedia of Psychology* Vol 2, Search Press, London.

Festinger, L. (1957) *A Theory of Cognitive Dissonance* Row Peterson, Evanston, Ill.

Fishbein, M. and Ajzen I. (1975) *Belief, Attitude, Intention and Behaviour* Addison-Wesley Publishing Co, Reading, Mass.

Gilson, E. (1957) *Painting and Reality* Pantheon Books Inc, New York.

Pincus, A and Minahan, A. (1973) *Social Work Practice: Model and Method* F E Peacock Publishers Inc, Itasca, Ill.

Poniatowski, M. (1986) *Les Technologies Nouvelles* Plon, Paris.

Sartre, J.-P. (1972) Plaidoyer pour les intellectuels. In *Situations* VIII, Gallimard, Paris.

Valéry, P. (1973) The idea of art. In Osborne, H. (ed) *Aesthetics* Oxford University Press.

Westley, B. and MacLean, M. (1957) A Conceptual Model for Communication Research, in *Journalism Quarterly* 34.

Wright Mills, C. (1959) *The Sociological Imagination* Penguin Books, Harmondsworth.

Appendix
Principles Discussed in
this Book

Note: In this book, the term 'principle' is defined as 'a generality derived from observation and assumed to be true.'

1. Public relations functions as a technology rather than a science (page 5).
2. A rational approach to public relations planning provides the strongest assurance of effectiveness (page 9).
3. A systematic approach to public relations planning lends itself to measuring progress (page 9).
4. Public relations is a management function (page 12).
5. Effective public relations is effective communication (page 14).
6. External public relations contracts are required only when the demands of a task go beyond the strengths and mix of in-house resources (page 21).
7. The public relations practitioner supports his client as much as possible and continually tries to promote his best interests (page 26).
8. In public relations, sociological surveys are carried out only by properly trained people (page 28).
9. To determine the opinion of a given public on a specific question, either a survey is commissioned or reference is made to a reliable and relevant one that has already been carried out (page 32).
10. Public relations seeks to establish and maintain mutual understanding between an organization and its publics (page 35).
11. Public relations goals clearly and absolutely contribute to overall organization objectives (page 35).
12. Public relations objectives never impede the attainment of any more important organization objectives (page 38).
13. Public relations contributes demonstrably to the attainment of any one or more of an organization's objectives (page 38).

14. Public relations contributes inevitably to the socio-cultural environment in which it operates (page 43).
15. In public relations, each public is considered separately and as many individually styled relationships as are necessary are established (page 47).
16. In public relations project proposals the logical connections between intermediate and final objectives are explicitly stated (page 57).
17. Public relations projects are always pretested before full implementation (page 65).
18. A proposition will be accepted only if it is compatible with the strongest dispositions of the public to which it is submitted (page 67).
19. The intellectual and emotional dimensions of attitudes, although closely linked, are separate factors, each having its own determinants (page 71).
20. The transition from a favourable attitude to an intention to act demands clear and precise direction (page 72).
21. In public relations, the preferred channel of communication is the one that most effectively reaches the public for whom a message is intended (page 79).
22. A continuing public information programme is always linked to sound performance (page 85).
23. In planning a public relations project one structures it with an eye to later evaluation (page 89).
24. In using symbols in public relations, one assesses the degree to which one's interpretation of them is shared (page 93).
25. In using symbols in public relations, one makes sure that the symbolism is reasonably stable, not shifting towards significant change (page 93).
26. The Action Plan spells out in concrete terms the requirements and implications of everything the rest of the plan proposes in ideal terms (page 93).
27. Both in projects and continuing programmes public relations budgeting is based on cost-benefit analysis (page 99).
28. Summative evaluation is designed to draw from a particular project all the kinds of information needed by an organization to maintain its self-steering capacity (page 107).
29. Formative evaluation provides, in a continuous way, all the kinds of information needed by an organization in both projects and continuing programmes (page 107).
30. Scientific, evaluative research is carried out only by people properly trained to do it (page 108).

31. The importance of public relations project and programme evaluation is absolute (page 110).
32. The requirements of the relationships between certain types of organization and certain publics determine the need for specialization (page 112).

Index

integrated model 52-5
intellectual dimension 68, 71
intellectuals 14-16
intention 71-3
  non-persistence of 73-4
  partial persistence of 73
  persistence 73
intermediate organization
  objectives 38
intermediate project objectives 8,
  38, 55-6, 93, 101
international religious organizations
  117, 119
interpersonal communication 76,
  78-9, 86
interval scale 41, 42
intuitive approach 10-11
irrational approach 10

job description 95, 97-8
jobs 95
journalism 131
journalists 30-2
jurisdiction, levels of 119

knowledge 61, 68

labour 100
lag 19
language 116-17
learning model 18, 19-20
logic 57
logical connections 56-7, 60

management 6, 25, 34, 39, 46, 93-4,
  132
  channels of communication in 95
  function 12-14
  mentality 38, 39, 40, 123
  standards 108
managers, of arts 126
marketing 7, 36-7
mass 48-9
mass communication, sociology of
  131
mass media 15, 44, 45, 76-81, 83
materials 101
  new 129
measurable costs 100
measurable goals 38, 40
measurement difficulties 100
measurement scales 41-2
measuring attitudes 42-3
memorization 66

memory 19
messages, repetition of 71
middle class 44-5
morals, standards of 108, 116
mutual understanding 7, 24, 34-5, 40,
  123, 129-30

national religious organizations
  117
necessary elements 87-8
neutrality 22-3
new industries 130
new materials 129
news media, purpose of 80-81
newspapers 80-83
news release, purpose of 81-2
new technologies 5, 129-30
nominal scale 41
non-rational approach 10-11

objectives
  justification of 8, 56-7
  unmeasurable 43-6
objectivity 21-2
one-way communication 79
on-going costs 100-1
open house 87-8
operational
  plan 9
  principles vii
  style 13-14
opinion leaders 29-32, 63
ordinal scale 41-2
organization 95-6
  function 112
  memory 19, 104, 106, 109
  need 82
  objectives 35-6, 37-8
  policies 112
  portrait 34, 39, 112
  structure 112, 117
organizations
  religious 117-18
    structure of 117, 120
  voluntary 113-17
out-of-pocket costs 100-1

partial images 34, 39
performance standards 108
persuasion, process of 61-2
persuasive communication 61-2, 65
  71-2, 75, 131
phasing 8, 94-5
planning vii, 8, 47 *ff*

143

policy
  formation 60
  statements 95, 98
political
  institutions 130
  judgement 23-4
  science 4, 132
possible elements 88
power 20, 25, 44
power structure 54
PR
  cultural context of vii, 29
  definition of 6
  image of 15-16
  nature of 1-16
  principles of vii, 3-5
  practitioners of 6
  process of 7-8
  social context of vii, 29
  social impact of 43-6
  training for viii, 131-3
  university training of 131
PR apprenticeship 113
PR, financial 113
PR, government 132
PR, in-house 21, 26
PR training
  basic courses in 131-3
  breadth in 131
  cultural context of vii, 29
  depth in 131-3
  university 131
press conference 79
press release 79, 81-2
pretest 65
print media 78
proactive PR 17-21
  information for 20-21, 104
probability 1-4, 58-9
problem identification 17, 23
project
  costs 100
  document 94, 101
  management 95-8
    objectives in 8, 33, 38, 55-6,
      93, 101
promotion 7, 36
psychology 4, 132
public
  acceptance 33
  information 85-6, 100
  interest 82
  merit 83-4
  need 81-2

opinion, articulation of 31
  participation 87-9
  perception 33-4
  service 80-81
  values 44-5
publicity 36, 83-5
publics 6, 22, 35, 47-55, 111-12, 120
  identification of 47-50, 55
  special-interest 111

qualitative
  information 46, 107
  objectives 43, 45-6
quality standards 108
quantification 13, 40, 43, 100
quantitative
  information 107
  objectives 43
  standards 109
questionnaires 28-9, 107

rational approach 9, 10
ratio scale 41, 42
reactive PR 17-18
reality and symbols 91
reference, terms of 12-13
relationships 3, 4, 60-61
  establishment of 75
religious
  belief 122
  organizations 117-18
    structure of 117, 120
  practice 121, 123
    traditional 123-4
research 4-5, 17-18, 27-9, 107
  methods of 2, 5, 27-9, 131
resources 17, 19, 40, 94, 98, 109, 119
responsive information 84-5
Roman Catholic Church 123-4

sampling 28
scheduling 8, 93-4
science 3-4, 5
scientific
  approach 2-3
  principles 3-5
second-hand information 29-30
selective attention 62-3
self-steering system 18-21, 27, 39-40,
  103-5, 107
semiotics 91, 131
similarity 70-71
situation analysis vii, 2, 7-8, 17-18,
  21, 23, 26, 104, 107

skeleton event 87-9
sleeper effect 73
social
   change 131, 132
   class 44-5
   ethics 111
   groups 47-9
   relationships 130
   sciences 11
   structures 5, 131
   worker 52-3
Society, The 121-4
sociological
   research 27-9
   skills 131
   surveys 27-9, 107
sociology 4, 5
special events 86-9
special-interest publics 111
specialized PR viii, 111-13
stability, levels of 67
standards 108
   of discipline 108
   of morals 108, 116
   performance 108
statistical
   analysis 131
   significance 29
steady-state system 18, 103
strategic plan 9
structural diagram 95-6
summative evaluation 9, 106

symbol 89-93
systematic approach 2-4, 7-9, 12
systems description 95, 98

Target Public 53-5
technological change 130
technologies, new 5, 129-30
technologist 4-5
technology 4-5, 111
testing hypotheses 2-4
timing 94-5
total cost 101
trademarks 92
traditional religious practice 123-4
truth 58
two-step flow 31
two-way communication 35, 79

uncertainty 1, 63
unemployment 129
unmeasurable objectives 43-6
useful information 63
utilitarian values 126

value judgement 23-4
values 115-16, 131
   conflict of 24
   promotion of 113
   utilitarian 126
voluntary organizations 113-17

Westley and MacLean model 81